NEW DIRECTIONS FOR STUDENT SERVICES

John H. Schuh, *Iowa State University*
EDITOR-IN-CHIEF

Elizabeth J. Whitt, *University of Iowa*
ASSOCIATE EDITOR

Serving Students with Disabilities

Holley A. Belch
Indiana University of Pennsylvania

EDITOR

Number 91, Fall 2000

JOSSEY-BASS PUBLISHERS
San Francisco

SERVING STUDENTS WITH DISABILITIES
Holley A. Belch (ed.)
New Directions for Student Services, no. 91
John H. Schuh, Editor-in-Chief
Elizabeth J. Whitt, Associate Editor

Microfilm copies of issues and articles are available in 16mm and 35mm, as well as microfiche in 105mm, through University Microfilms Inc., 300 North Zeeb Road, Ann Arbor, Michigan 48106-1346.

Persons who are unable to use standard printed material because of visual or physical disabilities should contact the National Library Services for the Blind and Physically Handicapped (NLS), a division of the Library of Congress, at 202-707-9275 (voice) or 202-707-0744 (TTY) for assistance in obtaining this work in an alternative format. Jossey-Bass will cooperate fully with the NLS and its associated libraries in making this volume available to users with special needs.

ISSN 0164-7970   ISBN 0-7879-5444-6

NEW DIRECTIONS FOR STUDENT SERVICES is part of The Jossey-Bass Higher and Adult Education Series and is published quarterly by Jossey-Bass Inc., Publishers, 350 Sansome Street, San Francisco, California 94104-1342. Periodicals postage paid at San Francisco, California, and at additional mailing offices. Postmaster: Send address changes to New Directions for Student Services, Jossey-Bass Inc., Publishers, 350 Sansome Street, San Francisco, California 94104-1342.

NEW DIRECTIONS FOR STUDENT SERVICES is indexed in College Student Personnel Abstracts and Contents Pages in Education.

SUBSCRIPTIONS cost $58.00 for individuals and $104.00 for institutions, agencies, and libraries. See ordering information page at end of book.

EDITORIAL CORRESPONDENCE should be sent to the Editor-in-Chief, John H. Schuh, N 243 Lagomarcino Hall, Iowa State University, Ames, Iowa 50011

Cover photograph by Wernher Krutein/PHOTOVAULT © 1990.

Jossey-Bass Web address: www.josseybass.com

Manufactured in the United States of America on acid-free recycled paper containing 100 percent recovered waste paper, of which at least 20 percent is postconsumer waste.

CONTENTS

EDITOR'S NOTES

This volume provides the higher education community generally and the student affairs profession specifically an opportunity to consider key issues that affect the growing population of students with disabilities. The chapter authors address not only two common concerns, legal requirements and architectural barriers, but also issues of dignity, access and meaningful participation, dimensions of inclusive and supportive environments, institutional obligations for recruitment and admissions, the value of and inclusion in out-of-class activities, strategies for career and academic advising, and the impact of financial resources on funding programs and services. Historically, the focus of the higher education community has been accommodations involving the location and level of access to assigned classrooms and residence halls, as well as academic requirements and, recently, learning accommodations.

New questions have emerged, however, that challenge us to look beyond the letter of the law to the spirit of the law and the essence of meaningful access and full participation. In the past, we were concerned with how students with physical, hearing, speech, or visual disabilities negotiate the physical aspects of the campus. Now we must consider how student affairs professionals, administrators, and faculty members can assist students with disabilities to gain meaningful access to and become full participants in a quality education.

Core values of community, equality, and human dignity serve as an important guiding influence for this volume. These values were proclaimed in the seminal historical documents of the student affairs profession in the form of honoring the uniqueness of the individual, maintaining a holistic view of the development of each student, serving the needs of a broad spectrum of students, and creating community among faculty, staff, and students by working in collaboration on behalf of student learning (American Council on Education, [1937] 1986a, [1949] 1986b).

Community as a value refers to the connection that embraces us as individuals, focuses our attention, and guides us through the educational process (Roberts, 1993). It is the synergy created by the collective effort of individuals to engage each other, to be willing to do something differently, or to learn something new in order to assist others in reaching their educational goals. Shaping and building community is an ongoing process that involves creating an environment that is inclusive and affirming of the uniqueness of individuals.

Equality as a value can be viewed as on a continuum (Clement, 1993). At one extreme is equality of opportunity, where opportunity should be equal for all with similar ability and aspirations regardless of social class. The random assignment of roommates in residence halls without regard to race, religion, or ethnicity serves as an example of equality of opportunity. At the other end of the continuum, fair opportunity describes equality in which intentional interventions mediate the effects of discrimination, bias, or inequity. Clement (1993) offered disability support programs as but one example of fair opportunity.

At the core of the struggle over individual rights is the notion of human dignity (Clement, 1993). For individuals with disabilities, the concept of human dignity is especially salient. The increasing diversity on college campuses compels us to recognize and celebrate the inherent worth of individuals through our behavior, attitudes, and language.

As we think about the values of community, equality, and human dignity with regard to students with disabilities, we are compelled to consider not only our individual convictions but also the positions taken by the institutions in which we work. Student learning, both in class and out of class, cannot be reserved solely for students who learn in ways that we recognize, or are familiar with, or are comfortable with. Higher education, as a learning community, must also welcome and engage those who think and process information differently than many other students do; those who see and experience life in very visual ways and communicate in a more tactile manner than many of us do; those who experience the world in a nonvisual sense, listen keenly, and hear and sense far more than most of us can imagine; and those who physically move from place to place with their own sense of grace and fluidity more so than many others.

It is necessary to extend beyond the efforts and good intentions of individual staff, administrators, and faculty in demonstrating care, nurturance, and a welcoming attitude to individual students in order to create an inclusive and affirming environment. What makes a program, or one part of the college experience, or a particular campus environment more welcoming to a specific student than another? Yuker (1988) characterized the influence of environment on individuals with disabilities as "often a characteristic of the environment rather than of the individual, and those of you who are psychologists will be aware that one of the great psychologists, Kurt Lewin, said that behavior is the function of a person in an environment. . . . The person may have the disability but the environment produces the handicap" (p. 33).

Attention to the environment and its influence on student development continues to play a significant role in our literature, theory base, and day-to-day life on campuses. Throughout this volume, you will recognize familiar concepts (recruitment, out-of-class activities, recreation, study abroad, career and academic advising) that are framed to acknowledge the equality and human dignity of students with disabilities. In addition, you will discover environmental conditions of support and challenge (legal, financial, theoretical) that will help you create supportive and engaging environments that reinforce the notion of community.

In Chapter One, Linda Hall and Holley Belch consider the core values of the student affairs profession and the essential meaning of access for students with disabilities. The lessons we have learned from the emergence of other historically underrepresented groups of students on our campuses serve as examples as we consider the demographic trends of students with disabilities and their participation in higher education.

In Chapter Two, Carney Strange provides a theoretical approach to understanding the influence and impact of environmental factors on the ability of a student to thrive and achieve. Beyond offering a theoretical perspective, he examines ways in which student affairs professionals can create conditions that improve the opportunities for success for students with disabilities.

In Chapter Three, Barbara Palombi suggests the recruitment of students with disabilities as a conventional admissions activity. The emphasis of this chapter is on providing all potential applicants in the recruitment process with appropriate information regarding support services. This approach transmits a sense of care, inclusiveness, and value to applicants who have a disability without compelling them to disclose in order to obtain helpful information. She identifies key issues in evaluating the admissibility of applicants and provides strategies for recruitment.

In Chapter Four, Donna Johnson considers the impact of involvement in activities, study abroad, experiential learning, and recreation and sports for students with disabilities. Out-of-class involvement is a critical element in the success of all students, including students with disabilities. She describes strategies, policies, and programs that serve as exemplary models of involvement.

In Chapter Five, Betty Aune argues for the utilization of an interactional model of disability in the framework of student development theory as a foundation for service delivery in career and academic advising.

In Chapter Six, Jo Anne Simon addresses the legal issues inherent in providing services to students with disabilities. She describes the most timely and current legal decisions and issues affecting higher education in general and student affairs professionals in particular.

Finally, in Chapter Seven, James Rund and Tedde Scharf consider various funding strategies necessary to sustain disability support programs. Complexity in the management of financial resources is addressed at the federal, state, and local levels. Case examples illustrate a range of ways in which various types of institutions successfully create opportunity, meaningful access, and full participation.

Throughout this volume, authors use the term *students with disabilities* to describe a group of students who have emerged as an underrepresented population on college campuses. As authors, we recognize that a singular term such as this does not convey the breadth of the types of disability (such as learning, visual, hearing, orthopedic, motor, speech, psychiatric, health related, multiple disabilities) represented by students today. It does, however, transmit a sense of understanding of the population of students at the heart of our discussion. We take a lesson from our work with other underrepresented populations in acknowledging that there are general issues or concerns shared by the larger group that might be addressed differently based on subgroup distinctions.

With all of our students, we have an obligation not only to recognize their struggles but also to identify ways in which we can help them transform struggle into accomplishment, disappointment into satisfaction, and presence into participation. This volume offers a framework for readers to examine their role in facilitating the integration of students with disabilities into the institution and to assist institutional representatives in clarifying their commitment to community, equality, and human dignity.

The authors hope to challenge readers to examine the manner in which student affairs professionals, administrators, and faculty individually and collectively take responsibility for the education and development of students who happen to have disabilities. Our intent is not simply to extend the traditional boundaries and responsibilities of disability support programs and the accompanying professional staff. Rather our work here is intended to challenge and broaden our thinking on the value of community, equality, and human dignity and the role we play individually and institutionally in ensuring the involvement and success of students with disabilities in higher education.

References

American Council on Education. "The Student Personnel Point of View." In G. Saddlemire and A. Rentz (eds.), *Student Affairs: A Profession's Heritage*. Alexandria, Va.: American College Personnel Association, 1986a. (Originally published 1937.)
American Council on Education. "The Student Personnel Point of View." In G. Saddlemire and A. Rentz (eds.), *Student Affairs: A Profession's Heritage*. Alexandria, Va.: American College Personnel Association, 1986b. (Originally published 1949.)
Clement, L. M. "Equality, Human Dignity, and Altruism: The Caring Concerns." In R. B. Young (ed.), *Identifying and Implementing the Essential Values of the Profession*. New Directions for Student Services, no. 61. San Francisco: Jossey-Bass, 1993.
Roberts, D. C. "Community: The Value of Social Synergy." In R. B. Young (ed.), *Identifying and Implementing the Essential Values of the Profession*. New Directions for Student Services, no. 61. San Francisco: Jossey-Bass, 1993.
Yuker, H. E. *Attitudes Toward Persons with Disabilities*. New York: Springer, 1988.

Holley A. Belch
Editor

HOLLEY A. BELCH *is assistant professor, student affairs in higher education, at Indiana University of Pennsylvania in Indiana, Pennsylvania. She has served as a student affairs professional at Arizona State University, Babson College (Massachusetts), and Siena College (New York) and on the faculty at Southern Illinois University-Carbondale.*

1

Campus communities committed to providing meaningful access to students with disabilities reflect and learn from their history with other underrepresented groups, understand today's students with disabilities, and wholeheartedly embrace opportunities and challenges before them with solid grounding in the core values of our profession.

Setting the Context: Reconsidering the Principles of Full Participation and Meaningful Access for Students with Disabilities

Linda M. Hall, Holley A. Belch

A series of legislative mandates in the past thirty years created access to higher education for students with disabilities. Demographic trends confirm the efficacy of the laws with regard to access as an increasing number of students with disabilities are enrolling in postsecondary education. Coupled with an ever increasing number of students with disabilities on campuses is the diversity in the type of disability these students have. In spite of these trends, students with disabilities have been less than successful in participating fully in the college experience and in attaining a college degree.

Legal Mandates

When Section 504 of the Rehabilitation Act of 1973 was signed into law, higher education was required to take seriously its responsibility to accommodate the needs of students who are disabled. Colleges and universities have struggled ever since to understand their accountability for meeting the needs of this growing population.

Efforts to serve the educational needs of students with disabilities began more than 135 years ago when Abraham Lincoln signed legislation to provide funding for Gallaudet University, a liberal arts institution in Washington, D.C., created to provide higher education for students who are deaf. This legislation sent a message to the country and to higher education that those with disabilities are not "incapable of thinking, learning, or achieving" (Jarrow, 1993, p. 5). Nevertheless another hundred years passed before additional legislation confirmed the legal responsibility of colleges and universities to provide meaningful access to students with disabilities. Section 504 of the Rehabilitation Act of 1973 (reauthorized in 1992) was the first national civil rights legislation that provided equal access for people with disabilities to public and private postsecondary institutions that receive federal financial assistance. Following the 1973 act, four more years were needed to issue the regulations that implemented this act.

The Americans with Disabilities Act (ADA), signed into law in 1990, extended disability law from federally funded programs and institutions to those funded by state and local governments as well as private institutions. The ADA defined disability with respect to an individual as (a) a physical or mental impairment that substantially limits one or more major life activities, (b) a record of such impairments, or (c) being regarded as having such an impairment (42 USC 12101[2]). Since the 1973 legislation providing access to students with disabilities, additional types of disabilities have been identified and included within the law, which requires campuses to understand differences among students with disabilities and respond in new ways to a wider variety of student needs. The spirit of the law will continue to serve as our compass while the letter of the law continues to be clarified. Since the ADA was signed in 1990, the demographics involving students with disabilities have dramatically changed on campuses.

Demographic Trends in Education

Since the mid-1980s, researchers have forecast the entry of growing numbers of students with disabilities into higher education (Fichten, 1988; Wiseman, Emry, and Morgan, 1988). In 1985, Hodgkinson's *All One System* provided the educational community with a compelling statement of the demographic trends that would lead us into the new millennium. There is clear evidence that students with disabilities are represented in increasing numbers on college campuses and have a wide variety of disabilities that are often unseen or invisible (Henderson, 1999).

Participation Rates in Higher Education. Several studies have provided data regarding the participation of students with disabilities in higher education. Between 1986 and 1994, the percentage of individuals with disabilities, age sixteen or older, who reported attending college or completing a degree rose from 29 to 45 (U.S. Department of Education, 1996). A study in 1996 revealed that 6 percent of all undergraduates reported having a disability (National Center for Education Statistics, 1999). In a study conducted in 1998, approximately 9 percent of all entering college freshmen reported having a disability, a substantial increase from 1978, when less than 3 percent reported a disability (Henderson, 1999). The self-report options of disability by college freshmen in the 1998 study included speech, orthopedic, learning disability, health related, partially sighted or blind, and other. Categories from the 1996 study (learning, orthopedic, hearing, visual, speech, and other) were similar to but not exactly as those outlined in the 1998 study (National Center for Education Statistics, 1999).

Factors Contributing to the Increase. A number of factors have converged to contribute to the increasing number of students with disabilities on college campuses. Over the past twenty-five years, disability rates in the general population have increased due to demographic changes. Despite some of the change attributable to an aging population, the increase since 1990 is due to children and young adults with disabilities (Kaye, LaPlante, Carlson, and Wenger, 1996).

The proportion of school-age children with disabilities has risen continually since the 1930s (Anderton, Barrett, and Bogue, 1997). The U.S. Department of Education has reported that in recent years the number of young people age six to twenty-one with disabilities has increased at a greater rate than the general school enrollment (HEATH, 1999). Mainstreaming in secondary schools, efforts by institutions of higher education to increase facility and program accessibility, advances in medical technology, civil rights laws, and an understanding that higher education increases opportunities for employment and independence have contributed to the increasing number of students with disabilities pursuing postsecondary education (Fichten, 1988; Fichten, Bourdon, Amsel, and Fox, 1987; Flick-Hruska and Blythe, 1992). State laws and mandates for transition planning at an early stage have helped students and parents focus during high school and plan for college (Brinckerhoff, Shaw, and McGuire, 1993; Mangrum and Strichart, 1992). Modifications in secondary education (such as greater contact with teachers, more structured time, and more effective teaching techniques and skills) (Brinckerhoff, Shaw, and McGuire, 1993) and changes over time in society's perception of disability (Walling, 1996) have also contributed to the increase in numbers of students with disabilities enrolling in higher education. Advances in adaptive technology have offered individuals with a variety of disabilities (for example, visual, orthopedic, motor, hearing, learning, speech) greater independence, self-sufficiency, and access to information (Lazzaro, 1993). In addition, students with specific types of disability (such as speech and language impairments, specific learning disabilities, hearing or visual impairment) are more likely to graduate from high school than students with multiple disabilities or autism (HEATH, 1999).

Varying Types of Disability. Not only has higher education witnessed an increase in the number of students with disabilities over time, but the range of disabilities in the student population has expanded as well (Kroeger and Schuck, 1993b; Ryan and McCarthy, 1994). A decade ago partially sighted or blind was the most commonly reported disability among college freshmen; it was fourth in frequency of reporting in 1998 (Henderson, 1999). "Disabling conditions that are most prevalent today are more likely to be invisible (learning disabilities, health impairments, speech impairments, low vision, or loss of hearing) than obvious (deafness, orthopedic, blindness)" (Henderson, 1992, p. iii).

Rates of participation of students with disabilities in higher education vary according to disability (Fairweather and Shaver, 1990; Henderson, 1999). Among students reporting a disability, 41 percent reported a learning disability, 22 percent said they had other disabilities, 19 percent indicated they had a health-related disability, 13 percent indicated they were partially sighted or blind, 12 percent were hearing impaired, 9 percent had orthopedic or physical impairments, and 5 percent had speech impairments (Henderson, 1999). Students with sensory impairments (hearing, visual) showed the highest rates of participation in postsecondary education, whereas young adults with multiple impairments (for example, visual and hearing, speech and mobility) were least represented among the college-going population (Fairweather and Shaver, 1990; HEATH, 1999). One reason for the lack of documentation of students with multiple disabilities on college campuses is directly attributable to data-gathering techniques. In both of the most recent studies, response categories are discreet, and respondents are instructed to select all categories that apply, thus indicating specific types of disability rather than signifying multiple disabilities as a descriptive category (Henderson, 1999; National Center for Education Statistics, 1999).

Enrollment by Institutional Type. Enrollment in postsecondary education by students with disabilities also varies by type of institution. Public two-year institutions enroll more than half of all college students reporting a disability (National Center for Education Statistics, 1999; Phillippe, 1997); students with disabilities account for 8 percent of the total enrollment at two-year institutions (Barnett and Li, 1997; Phillippe, 1997). Enrollment of students with disabilities at four-year institutions is considerably lower than at two-year colleges, except among students with visual impairments (Fairweather and Shaver, 1990). Although enrollment of students with disabilities at four-year institutions has increased in the past decade (Henderson, 1999), most students with disabilities who enter two-year institutions are not transferring to a four-year institution and pursuing a baccalaureate degree (National Center for Education Statistics, 1999). Very little, if anything, is known as to why this is the case.

A revolving door has been created for many students of underrepresented groups (such as racial and ethnic minorities, women, older, and part time) who have entered higher education (Edwards, 1993); their ability to succeed in earning a degree is disappointing at best (Harris and Nettles, 1996). Among all enrolled students with disabilities, half earned a degree, compared with two-thirds of their nondisabled peers (National Center for Education Statistics, 1999). Students with disabilities, an underrepresented group, have a right to be part of higher education, and it appears that as a group they are affirming their desire to participate by virtue of the demographic trends. Increased campus diversity requires that we face head on the growing concerns of students with disabilities and respond in multiple ways to a wide variety of needs, issues, and student aspirations. Who better to respond than student affairs?

Values in Student Affairs

Of all the constituencies on college campuses, student affairs, by virtue of its historical commitment to differences and the espoused values of the profession, has assumed leadership for creating learning environments that are inclusive, diverse, and affirming. In doing so, values of human dignity, equality, and community serve as an appropriate framework for working with students.

Historical Commitment. Key documents heralding the philosophical tenets of working with students continue to serve as guiding assumptions for the student affairs profession. The Student Personnel Point of View (SPPV), a historically significant document, emphasized the obligation of educators to consider the student as a whole, unique individual—not only his or her intellectual development but also emotional and physical development, social relationships, vocational skills, and moral and religious values (American Council on Education, [1937] 1986a, [1949] 1986b). The fundamental elements of the Student Personnel Point of View—the holistic view of students, the acknowledgment and recognition of individual differences, and the confirmation of community—reflect the values of community, equality, and human dignity (American Council on Education, [1937] 1986a, [1949] 1986b; Clement, 1993; Young, 1993).

Differences in students can take many forms, and student affairs professionals have a responsibility to a wide variety of individuals capable of benefiting from higher education (Council of Student Personnel Associations, 1986). In the recent past, student affairs has been involved in responding to student differences and promoting diversity in a number of ways, including the programs developed on many campuses (Carreathers, Beekmann, Coatie, and Nelson, 1996; Levine, 1993; Terrell, 1992), published research, and student affairs scholarship (Levine, 1993; Pascarella and others, 1996), promoting understanding of diversity through national and regional student affairs conference themes and programs (Henley, Powell, and Poats, 1992) and efforts to diversify membership within professional associations (Patitu and Terrell, 1998). This list of activities suggests the commitment that many student affairs professionals have to promoting diverse campus environments and that the actions of many professionals are consistent with the espoused values of the profession and creating inclusive communities.

Espoused Values of Student Affairs. Although access to higher education for underrepresented groups can be viewed from a legal perspective, core values in student affairs provide an equally compelling moral lens from which to examine working with students. Values of community, human

dignity, and equality are more contemporary expressions of the longstanding historically important values of the work in student affairs (Young,
1993), and these values are worthy of reconsideration in working with students from underrepresented groups, specifically students with disabilities.

Community. Community making is the heritage of the student affairs
profession, and Roberts (1993) challenged professionals to develop and sustain community on their campuses. Community is a *place* where individuals can communicate honestly, authentic and intimate relationships are
established, and a commitment is developed to sharing joys and sorrows
together. Community emerges through the *process* of human interaction
(Roberts, 1993). The growing diversity on campuses creates an even greater
challenge in community building work. While understanding student differences may provide helpful and multiple perspectives, it is also important
to acknowledge that there are ways in which individual community
members are alike. As professionals seek to understand the needs of students with disabilities, it is valuable to recognize that those with disabilities
are more like others in campus communities than they are different (Nutter
and Ringgenberg, 1993; Jarrow, 1987). One way in which students are alike
is that all need to feel that they matter—to have a sense of belonging on
campus and to believe that others care and are concerned about them
(Schlossberg, Lynch, and Chickering, 1989). Students feel that they belong
when members of the campus community articulate verbally, in written
documents, and by their behavior, "We are glad you are here, we want to
know you, and we want you to be a part of what we do on this campus."
These positive and inclusive messages affect all, and for those who may feel
marginalized (as if they do not fully belong), as in the case of some students
with disabilities, clearly stated acceptance is especially important in order
to integrate students with disabilities into the academic community (Schuck
and Kroeger, 1993; Nutter and Ringgenberg, 1993).

Equality. The concept of equality, which focuses on groups as opposed
to individuals in campus communities, has been widely discussed and
debated within higher education (Clement, 1993). Members of underrepresented groups have fought for equal rights and opportunities in order to
be present and successful within institutions of higher education. Student
affairs professionals must both welcome students with disabilities to campuses and develop policies, programs, and services that improve opportunities for success for this underrepresented group. In embracing equality as a
value, however, one must be cognizant of the individual differences among
groups (such as students with disabilities) and account for differences mean-
ingfully into the design of programs and services (Clement, 1993).

Human Dignity. While the focus of equality is on groups, the focus of
human dignity is on individuals (Clement, 1993). Human dignity is
described as the individual's inherent self-worth and dignity (Young and
Elfrink, 1991) and involves others' ascribing worth to an individual,
acknowledging the basic worth of each person, and feeling personally wor-

thy (Clement, 1993). Numerous examples are found on most campuses where individual students' feelings of self-worth are threatened by the dehumanizing and depersonalizing behavior of others. Messages of being valued and personally worthy are important for everyone to experience, and in the case of students with disabilities, we need to honor individual identity, confront dehumanizing behavior, and clearly affirm the value of their involvement and what they bring to campus communities. Fundamentally, human dignity can be achieved by using person-first language that emphasizes the individual and not the disability. Language shapes attitudes, positively and negatively, and the importance of people-first language, that is, putting the person before the disability, cannot be underestimated in an educational setting (Guth and Murphy, 1998).

Values in Context. What do the values of community, equality, and human dignity look like in action and specifically in the context of working with students with disabilities? Have student affairs professionals encouraged skilled and interested students with hearing impairments to apply for peer adviser positions? Have we helped students with learning disabilities develop the skills to organize a campaign to run for an elected student government office? Have we actively solicited the participation and provided support to students with visual impairments to become involved in judicial boards? Have we provided the same level of advisement and support for students with disabilities as they work to establish a student organization as we might have for other student groups?

Although there is no clearly marked road map to help us navigate the unfamiliar territory as underrepresented groups have emerged on campuses, the values of community, equality, and human dignity can help guide the way. A commitment to these values positions student affairs professionals to assist students who need individual consideration in meeting their educational goals. Developing community and promoting dignity and equality for students with disabilities lead us to consider their needs, goals, and aspirations carefully and involve them in planning and evaluation efforts. Student affairs, in an important position to provide campus leadership in responding to these needs, is met with significant challenges.

Challenges Facing Student Affairs

Student affairs professionals face several challenges in approaching work with students with disabilities. Historically, underrepresented groups have found it difficult to feel that they are a valued part of the campus culture and acknowledged for the richness of experience and culture they bring to the community. Student affairs organizations have struggled with structures that are disjointed and fragmented, often making it difficult to provide a coordinated, comprehensive response. Student affairs professionals have been limited by their own tendencies to provide short-term programmatic solutions that fail to address long-term problems of policy and new practice.

They also find it difficult to devote adequate time to professional development and to internal communication and program collaboration.

Historical Response to Underrepresented Groups. The term *underrepresented* is often understood to include racial and ethnic minorities; however, the definition has been expanded to include women, students with disabilities, and other groups (such as part-time, older, and international students and students who are other than heterosexually oriented) (Patitu and Terrell, 1998). On many campuses, some of these groups are in the majority numerically, although this has not always been the case. There are many differences among these groups, but a common thread is that when each entered higher education, they found the environment unwelcoming (Clement, 1993; Jones, 1996; Levine, 1993).

Higher education has consistently responded to underrepresented student groups in ways that have been at best benign and at worst disaffirming. The response has not always been intentional; in many cases it has been inadvertent and at times was embedded in ignorance. In the case of students of color, McNairy (1996) pointed to an indifferent or hostile campus atmosphere, with limited professional role models, and social activities where students of color feel unwelcome. Women students found the campus climate "chilly" (Hall and Sandler, 1984), and as a result, higher education was challenged to develop an understanding of their differences from male students in order to establish policies and practices that responded to their needs. Part-time and older students point to nonacademic campus activities that are scheduled for evenings, when other responsibilities conflict with their ability to attend. Although the specific barriers have been different for different groups, the commonality illustrated by these examples has been some barrier to a welcoming and inclusive environment.

For decades, these groups have had legally established rights to enroll in institutions of higher education; however, on arrival they experienced various forms of discrimination or insensitivity and less than equal opportunities for success on some campuses (Allen, 1992; McNairy, 1996; Mow and Nettles, 1990). Many students with disabilities face the same predicament; they have encountered what has been termed "attitudinal access" challenges (Kroeger and Schuck, 1993a). They can enroll in colleges and universities, and those with mobility impairments may even find physical barriers surmountable on some campuses, but the attitudes of some in the campus community may create profound challenges to their ability to be successful (Kroeger and Schuck, 1993a). Students' personal development and learning increase as their involvement with the university environment increases (Astin, 1984); however, involvement might be difficult to achieve for those who encounter unwelcoming attitudes of exclusion or insensitivity.

Although a discouraging picture of the higher education experience of underrepresented students has been portrayed thus far, student affairs professionals have often championed efforts to welcome groups of historically underrepresented students and to provide leadership for diversity efforts (Levine, 1993). A challenge that student affairs professionals face is how to encourage others on campus to see diversity as an opportunity to shape an institution's future rather than to see it as a problem (Levine, 1993).

Influence of Organizational Structures. The organizational structures that student affairs has developed also have implications for how professionals identify their roles in relation to underrepresented students. The 1937 Student Personnel Point of View recommended program integration within student affairs, but practice during the past thirty years has become increasingly specialized and segregated (Schroeder, 1999). Among other factors, Schroeder suggested, increasingly diverse student populations have led institutions to create highly specialized hierarchical organizations that have led to "compartmentalization and fragmentation, often resulting in *functional silos* or *mine shafts*" (p. 9). On many campuses, offices or centers for underrepresented groups have been created (for example, cultural and women's centers, international student offices, and disability services offices). These programs help students to feel comfort and that they matter to the institution (Harris and Nettles, 1996; Nutter and Ringgenberg, 1993). However, student affairs professionals need to consider if, as an unintended consequence, special programs and centers also relieve staff who are not located in those centers from acting on their responsibility to understand and address the diverse needs of underrepresented groups. The same concern potentially arises when student affairs departments designate an individual staff member as liaison to a special program—in this case, the disabilities services office. The liaison should not be the only person to provide services to students with disabilities (Nutter and Ringgenberg, 1993). It must be a shared and collaborative responsibility.

While there is a mix between models of centralized and decentralized programs for students with disabilities (Schuck and Kroeger, 1993), a coordinated approach to service delivery is essential in an effective student affairs organization that serves the needs of students with disabilities (Nutter and Ringgenberg, 1993). Knowledge of specific disabilities, understanding of institutional barriers, advocacy, and an ongoing dialogue about learning opportunities for students with disabilities must be part of the agenda for all student affairs professionals and faculty members (Nutter and Ringgenberg, 1993).

Limitations as "Doers." Student affairs professionals value "doing" over thinking and reflecting (Love and others, 1993). While this preference to be doers has provided diversity initiatives on many campuses, it may also get in the way of spending time reading and making thoughtful conceptual connections. A renewed commitment to time spent in thinking and reflecting may lead student affairs professionals to provide an improved learning environment for underrepresented students, specifically students with disabilities, and more thoughtful consideration of programs, policies, and practices in the light of their needs.

Hiring Practices. Staff members with disabilities should be present on campuses (Belch, 1994; Shuford, 1998). If efforts are not made to hire professional staff who have disabilities, opportunities are lost to enhance diversity, provide role models for students with disabilities, and learn alongside others by engaging in dialogue regarding the challenges in providing individualized and flexible programs on campuses. If professionals with disabilities are not present among the staff, a message of exclusion may be sent to students and other community members, a message that conflicts with the values of community, equality, and human dignity.

Student affairs staff face these and other challenges in providing responsive services, programs, and policies for underrepresented groups, including students with disabilities. In spite of these challenges, student affairs has acted on longstanding values of the profession. Levine (1993) found that student affairs was the campus division that was most involved in turning the "rhetoric of diversity into reality" (p. 337).

Conclusion

Despite the demographic transformation of the student population and lack of clarity in interpreting the law regarding students with disabilities, the student affairs profession is positioned to respond to the needs of these students. It is important to acknowledge, however, that significant tasks remain for higher education in general and student affairs in particular in order to change the experience of students with disabilities.

The chapter authors in this volume identify the tasks and challenges of meeting the goals of inclusion, security, and involvement of students with disabilities in higher education. The tasks are not insurmountable yet require careful thought and consideration. Ideas, workable solutions, and examples of successful strategies are offered in the following chapters to assist student affairs professionals, faculty, and staff in their work with students with disabilities.

References

Allen, W. R. "The Color of Success: African-American College Student Outcomes at Predominantly White and Historically Black Public Colleges and Universities." *Harvard Educational Review,* 1992, 62, 26–44.

American Council on Education. "The Student Personnel Point of View." In G. Saddlemire and A. Rentz (eds.), *Student Affairs: A Profession's Heritage.* Alexandria, Va.: American College Personnel Association, 1986a. (Originally published 1937.)

American Council on Education. "The Student Personnel Point of View." In G. Saddlemire and A. Rentz (eds.), *Student Affairs: A Profession's Heritage.* Alexandria, Va.: American College Personnel Association, 1986b. (Originally published 1949.)

Americans with Disabilities Act of 1990. Public Law 101-336, 42 U.S.C., 12101–12132.

Anderton, D. L., Barrett, R. E., and Bogue, D. J. *The Population of the United States.* (3rd ed.) New York: Free Press, 1997.

Astin, A. W. "Student Involvement: A Developmental Theory for Higher Education." *Journal of College Student Personnel,* 1984, *25,* 297–308.

Barnett, L., and Li, Y. *Disability Support Services in Community Colleges* (Research Brief ACC-RB-97-1). Washington, D.C.: American Association of Community Colleges, 1997.

Belch, H. A. "Professionals with Disabilities." In D. Ryan and M. McCarthy (eds.), *A Student Affairs Guide to the Americans with Disabilities Act and Disability Issues.* Washington, D.C.: National Association of Student Personnel Administrators, 1994.

Brinckerhoff, L. C., Shaw, S. F., and McGuire, J. M. *Promoting Postsecondary Education for Students with Learning Disabilities: A Handbook for Practitioners.* Austin, Tex.: Pro-Ed, 1993.

Carreathers, K. R., Beekmann, L., Coatie, R. M., and Nelson, W. L. "Three Exemplary Retention Programs." In I. H. Johnson and A. J. Ottens (eds.), *Leveling the Playing Field: Promoting Academic Success for Students of Color.* New Directions for Student Services, no. 74. San Francisco: Jossey-Bass, 1996.

Clement, L. M. "Equality, Human Dignity, and Altruism: The Caring Concerns." In R. B. Young (ed.), *Identifying and Implementing the Essential Values of the Profession.* New Directions for Student Services, no. 61. San Francisco: Jossey-Bass, 1993.

Council of Student Personnel Associations. "Student Development Services in Postsecondary Education." In G. Saddlemire and A. Rentz (eds.), *Student Affairs: A Profession's Heritage.* Alexandria, Va.: American College Personnel Association, 1986.

Edwards, F. M. "Behind the Open Door: Disadvantaged Students." In A. Levine (ed.), *Higher Learning in America 1980–2000.* Baltimore: Johns Hopkins University Press, 1993.

Fairweather, J. S., and Shaver, D. M. "A Troubled Future? Participants in Postsecondary Education by Youths with Disabilities." *Journal of Higher Education,* 1990, *61*(3), 332–349.

Fichten, C. S. "Students with Physical Disabilities in Higher Education: Attitudes and Beliefs That Affect Integration." In H. E. Yuker (ed.), *Attitudes Toward Persons with Disabilities.* New York: Springer, 1988.

Fichten, C. S., Bourdon, C. V., Amsel, R., and Fox, L. "Validation of the College Interaction Self-Efficacy Questionnaire: Students with and Without Disabilities." *Journal of College Student Personnel,* 1987, *28*(5), 449–458.

Flick-Hruska, C., and Blythe, G. *Disability Accommodation Handbook.* Kansas City, Mo.: Metropolitan Community Colleges, 1992. (ED 358 880)

Guth, L. J., and Murphy, L. "People First Language in Middle and High Schools: Usability and Readability." *Clearing House,* 1998, *72,* 115–117.

Hall, R. M., and Sandler, B. R. *Out of the Classroom: A Chilly Campus Climate for Women: Report of the Project on the Status and Education of Women.* Washington, D.C.: Association of American Colleges, 1984.

Harris, S. M., and Nettles, M. T. "Ensuring Campus Climates That Embrace Diversity." In L. I. Rendon and R. O. Hope (eds.), *Educating a New Majority: Transforming America's Educational System for Diversity.* San Francisco: Jossey-Bass, 1996.

HEATH. *Facts You Can Use: Basis of Exit from High School Special Education for Students with Disabilities, Ages 17–21.* Washington, D.C.: American Council on Education, HEATH Resource Center, 1999.

Henderson, C. *College Freshmen with Disabilities.* Washington, D.C.: American Council on Education, 1992.

Henderson, C. *College Freshmen with Disabilities: A Biennial Statistical Profile.* Washington, D.C.: American Council on Education, HEATH Resource Center, 1999.

Henley, B., Powell, T., and Poats, L. "Achieving Cultural Diversity." In M. C. Terrell (ed.), *Diversity, Disunity, and Campus Community.* Washington, D.C.: National Association of Student Personnel Administrators, 1992.

Hodgkinson, H. *All One System: Demographics of Education, Kindergarten Through Graduate School.* Washington, D.C.: Institute of Educational Leadership, 1985. (ED 261 101)

Jarrow, J. E. "Integration of Individuals with Disabilities in Higher Education: A Review of the Literature." *Journal of Postsecondary Education and Disability*, 1987, 5(2), 38–57.

Jarrow, J. "Beyond Ramps: New Ways of Viewing Access." In S. Kroeger and J. Schuck (eds.), *Responding to Disability Issues in Student Affairs*. New Directions for Student Services, no. 64. San Francisco: Jossey-Bass, 1993.

Jones, S. R. "Toward Inclusive Theory: Disability as Social Construction." *NASPA Journal*, 1996, 33, 347–354.

Kaye, H. S., LaPlante, M. P., Carlson, D., and Wenger, B. L. *Trends in Disability Rates in the United States, 1970–1994*. Disability Statistics Abstract, no. 17. Washington, D.C.: National Institute on Disability and Rehabilitation Research, 1996.

Kroeger, S., and Schuck, J. "Moving Ahead: Issues, Recommendations, and Conclusions." In S. Kroeger and J. Schuck (eds.), *Responding to Disability Issues in Student Affairs*. New Directions for Student Services, no. 64. San Francisco: Jossey-Bass, 1993a.

Kroeger, S., and Schuck, J. (eds.). "Editor's Notes." In S. Kroeger and J. Schuck (eds.), *Responding to Disability Issues in Student Affairs*. New Directions for Student Services, no. 64. San Francisco: Jossey-Bass, 1993b.

Lazzaro, J. J. *Adaptive Technologies for Learning and Work Environments*. Chicago: American Library Association, 1993.

Levine, A. "Diversity on Campus." In A. Levine (ed.), *Higher Learning in America, 1980–2000*. Baltimore: Johns Hopkins University Press, 1993.

Love, P. G., and others. "Student Culture." In G. D. Kuh (ed.), *Cultural Perspectives in Student Affairs Work*. Washington, D.C.: American College Personnel Association, 1993.

Mangrum, C. T., and Strichart, S. S. (eds.). *Peterson's Guide to Colleges with Programs for Students with Learning Disabilities*. (3rd ed.) Princeton, N.J.: Peterson's Guides, 1992.

McNairy, F. G. "The Challenge for Higher Education: Retaining Students of Color." In I. H. Johnson and A. J. Ottens (eds.), *Leveling the Playing Field: Promoting Academic Success for Students of Color*. New Directions for Student Services, no. 74. San Francisco: Jossey-Bass, 1996.

Mow, S. L., and Nettles, M. T. "Minority Student Access to, and Persistence and Performance in, College: A Review of the Trends and Research Literature." In J. Smart (ed.), *The Handbook of Higher Education*. New York: Agathon Press, 1990.

National Center for Education Statistics. *Students with Disabilities in Postsecondary Education*. Washington, D.C.: National Center for Education Statistics, U.S. Department of Education, 1999.

Nutter, K. J., and Ringgenberg, L. J. "Creating Positive Outcomes for Students with Disabilities." In S. Kroeger and J. Schuck (eds.), *Responding to Disability Issues in Student Affairs*. New Directions for Student Services, no. 64. San Francisco: Jossey-Bass, 1993.

Pascarella, E. T., and others. "What Have We Learned from the First Year of the National Study of Student Learning?" *Journal of College Student Development*, 1996, 37(2) 182–192.

Patitu, C. L., and Terrell, M. C. "Benefits of Affirmative Action in Student Affairs." In D. D. Gehring (ed.), *Responding to the New Affirmative Action Climate*. New Directions for Student Services, no. 83. San Francisco: Jossey-Bass, 1998.

Phillippe, K. *National Profile of Community Colleges: Trends and Statistics, 1997–1998*. Washington, D.C.: American Association of Community Colleges, 1997.

Roberts, D. C. "Community: The Value of Social Synergy." In R. B. Young (ed.), *Identifying and Implementing the Essential Values of the Profession*. New Directions for Student Services, no. 61. San Francisco: Jossey-Bass, 1993.

Ryan, D., and M. McCarthy (eds.). "Introduction." In *A Student Affairs Guide to the Americans with Disabilities Act and Disability Issues*. Washington, D.C.: National Association of Student Personnel Administrators, 1994.

Schlossberg, N. K., Lynch, A. Q., and Chickering, A. W. *Improving Higher Education Environments for Adults: Responsive Programs and Services from Entry to Departure*. San Francisco: Jossey-Bass, 1989.

Schroeder, C. "Partnerships: An Imperative for Enhancing Student Learning and Institutional Effectiveness." In J. H. Schuh and E. J. Whitt (eds.), *Creating Successful Partnerships Between Academic and Student Affairs.* New Directions for Student Services, no. 87. San Francisco: Jossey-Bass, 1999.

Schuck, J., and Kroeger, S. "Essential Elements in Effective Service Delivery." In S. Kroeger and J. Schuck (eds.), *Responding to Disability Issues in Student Affairs.* New Directions for Student Services, no. 64. San Francisco: Jossey-Bass, 1993.

Shuford, B. C. "Recommendations for the Future." In D. D. Gehring (ed.), *Responding to the New Affirmative Action Climate.* New Directions for Student Services, no. 83. San Francisco: Jossey-Bass, 1998.

Terrell, M. C. (ed.). *Diversity, Disunity, and Campus Community.* Washington, D.C.: National Association of Student Personnel Administrators, 1992.

U.S. Department of Education. *Eighteenth Annual Report to Congress of Persons with Disabilities.* Washington, D.C.: U.S. Department of Education, 1996.

Walling, L. L. *Hidden Abilities in Higher Education: New College Students with Disabilities.* Columbia, S.C.: National Resource Center for the Freshman Year Experience, 1996.

Wiseman, R. L., Emry, R. A., and Morgan, D. "Predicting Academic Success for Disabled Students in Higher Education." *Research in Higher Education,* 1988, 28(3), 255–269.

Young, R. B. "The Essential Values of the Profession." In R. B. Young (ed.), *Identifying and Implementing the Essential Values of the Profession.* New Directions for Student Services, no. 61. San Francisco: Jossey-Bass, 1993.

Young, R. B., and Elfrink, V. L. "Essential Values of Student Affairs Work." *Journal of College Student Development,* 1991, 32(1), 47–55.

LINDA M. HALL is associate professor, student affairs in higher education, at Indiana University of Pennsylvania in Indiana, Pennsylvania.

HOLLEY A. BELCH is assistant professor, student affairs in higher education, at Indiana University of Pennsylvania in Indiana, Pennsylvania.

2

Environments of ability include, secure, involve, and engage all students in a learning community.

Creating Environments of Ability

Carney Strange

Campus discussions of disability inevitably turn to images of students who use wheelchairs negotiating a maze of curb cuts and out-of-reach counter-tops, along with insistent offers, from able-bodied, well-meaning peers, faculty, or staff, of "Here, let me help!" The expanding enrollment of students with disabilities of all kinds at American colleges and universities presents a significant challenge, for both those whose disabilities shape their experiences on campus in challenging ways and those who seek to include them. Of concern to all is how the postsecondary community views these students and responds to their needs.

Jones (1996) identified three "prevailing theoretical frameworks for understanding students with disabilities" (p. 348). First, from a "functional limitations framework," each affected student is viewed as having a disabling condition, and this biological fact "[governs] the student's sense of self, [explains] all problems experienced by the student, and [renders] the student in need of help and support" (Jones, 1996, p. 349). (Also see Fine and Asch, 1988, and Hahn, 1991.) Implied in this view is the need to rehabilitate the individual as the remedy to challenges of disability. A second framework is the "minority group paradigm," which focuses on issues of "alienation, marginalization, discrimination, and oppression" (Jones, 1996, p. 349). Accordingly, students with disabilities "may not be understood fully without considering consequences of minority group status, privilege, and the disabling environment" (p. 350). A remedy to exclusion is found in group solidarity, political action, and institutional advocacy. The third framework, "social constructivism," emerges from an understanding that "much of what is believed about disability results from meanings attached by those who are not disabled and challenges the assumptions upon which those meanings rest" (p. 350). The social constructivist remedy to challenges of disability entails consciousness raising, of those who experience as well as those who observe disabilities, and exposing of oppressive social structures that have "created handicaps out of characteristics" (p. 351).

Whereas the functional and minority group frameworks focus on the individual or collective condition of the disabled student, the social constructivist position "shifts [the] analysis from one focusing on the disability itself to one recognizing the intersection of individual and societal factors" (Jones, 1996, p. 348). This last perspective, first articulated by Lewin (1936) in his classic formula—that behavior results from the interaction between the person and the environment—reflects a more complex view of human behavior than one from a personal or environmental perspective alone, and it requires an understanding of the interactions of students and their campus environments. Educators need to understand not only the conditions and characteristics of students with disabilities but also the conditions and characteristics of the campus environments these students inhabit. To do so requires an understanding of the various dimensions that compose any environment, as well as how these dimensions might serve institutions dedicated to educational purposes and responsive to the concerns of students with disabilities.

Environmental Components

Key components of all human environments are their physical design and layout, the characteristics of people who inhabit them, the organizational structures related to their purposes and goals, and inhabitants' collective social constructions of the prevailing press, social climate, and culture (Moos, 1986; Strange and Banning, 2000). These four sets of components—physical, human aggregate, organizational, and socially constructed—can assist educators and advisers of students with disabilities in understanding the essential characteristics of colleges and universities that, in turn, shape the experiences and outcomes for these students.

Physical. The physical components of campus environments, both natural (the weather) and synthetic (interior color schemes), shape attitudes toward and influence experiences in institutions in powerful ways (Stern, 1986; Sturner, 1973; Thelin and Yankovich, 1987), serving both functional and symbolic ends. They define space for activities, functions, and events, thereby encouraging some phenomena while limiting others (Michelson, 1970). For example, a classroom with movable chairs might facilitate small group discussions more readily than one with furniture fixed to the floor. Physical components also send symbolic, nonverbal messages. A teaching podium placed twenty feet from the first row of seats might signal the formal nature of an impending classroom experience. Physical artifacts, such as signs, art work, posters, and graffiti, that are placed on campus to direct, inspire, or warn (Banning and Bartels, 1993) also send strong nonverbal messages about campus culture, which are often seen as more truthful than written or verbal messages (Mehrabian, 1981). The best outcomes result when physical components, both functional and symbolic, support desired behaviors consistently (Wicker, 1984).

Human Aggregate. Human aggregate components are those related to the collective characteristics of people in an environment. Whether demographic (for example, sex, age, or race) or psychosocial (for example, personality types or learning styles), human aggregate characteristics create features in an environment that reflect varying degrees of differentiation (such as type homogeneity) and consistency (such as type similarity) (Holland, 1973; Smart, Feldman, and Ethington, 2000). An environment inhabited mostly by individuals of one characteristic or type is said to be highly differentiated and consistent. This would be the case with a class where all students share the same major or a residence hall where residents are of the same gender. An environment dominated by a single and consistent type accentuates its own characteristics over time (Astin, 1985), attracting, satisfying, and retaining individuals who share the dominant features. The quality of anyone's experience is therefore a function of his or her congruence, or degree of fit, with the dominant group. An individual placed in an incompatible environment is less likely to be reinforced for preferred behaviors, values, attitudes, and expectations, and the likelihood of that person's leaving the environment is increased. The experiences of cultural minorities on historically white campuses reflect these dynamics as students of color struggle to accommodate the preferences, values, attitudes, and expectations of the majority. Those who do not usually often leave the institution.

Organizational. Organizational components arise from the myriad decisions made about environmental purposes and functions. Who is in charge? How will resources be distributed? By what rules, if any, will those in the environment function? What must be accomplished and how quickly? How will participants be rewarded for their accomplishments? Getting organized is a typical response to such questions, generating various arrangements or structures that define the organizational characteristics of an environment. For example, concentrating decision-making power within a few individuals in the environment yields a high degree of centralization (Hage, 1980), just as a decision to enforce numerous explicit rules implies a high degree of formalization in the setting (Price, 1972). The importance of these organizational structures is that they converge to create characteristic organizational milieus, reflecting a continuum of flexibility (Hage and Aiken, 1970). At one end are dynamically organized environments, flexible in design, less centralized, and informal; at the other end are static environments, rigid, centralized, and formal. These milieus, in turn, affect the four performances of any successful organization, which are innovation, efficiency, quantity of production, and morale (Hage, 1980). Like all other organized environments, colleges and universities must innovate, produce efficiently, and maintain a modicum of satisfaction among those who participate in them. Whether an environment is able to achieve these performances is influenced by the degree to which it can maintain a dynamic quality and how well it can mitigate the effects of organizational size. In general, the larger the organization is, the more challenging it becomes to succeed at these goals.

Socially Constructed. Socially constructed components reflect the subjective views or social constructions of environmental participants. This perspective assumes that environments are understood best through people's collective perceptions of them, as manifested in environmental presses (or consensus about what behaviors the environment encourages and supports), social climates, and cultures. These perceptions in turn influence behavior in the environment. A distinctive environmental press is evident in any consensus of perceptions about particular behaviors or expectations. For example, perceptions that the majority of students on a particular campus work diligently in the library between classes and on weekends imply the presence of a press toward academic achievement. Environments can also be described in terms of their personalities, or social climates, composed of relationship, personal development and growth, and system maintenance and change dimensions (Moos, 1968, 1979). The personalities of two classroom environments can differ dramatically in, for example, the degree to which students are perceived to support one another (a relationship dimension), the goals and expectations of the course (a personal growth and development dimension), or the extent to which innovation and creativity are encouraged (a system maintenance and change dimension) (Moos and Trickett, 1974). Last, the culture of any environment reflects an amalgam of assumptions, beliefs, and values that inhabitants use to interpret or understand the meaning of events and actions (Schein, 1992). Thus environmental culture forms a distinctive character usually known only to members but leaves an impression on those from without who encounter it.

Summary of Components. An understanding of any human environment begins with the identification of its essential features—its physical components and design, its dominant human characteristics, the organizational structures that serve its purposes, and participants' constructions of its presses, social climate, and culture. These components create a variety of environmental conditions on campus, and enhance or detract from student learning and success (American College Personnel Association, 1994).

Environmental Goals and Purposes

Learning entails a progression of increasingly complex steps in meaning making and understanding, requiring both the acquisition of new information and opportunities for the exercise of new skills, competencies, and ways of thinking and acting. Learning merges personal identity, values, beliefs, knowledge, skills, and interests toward fulfillment and human actualization.

This conception is at the heart of the classic model of human development and motivation articulated by Maslow (1968). Maslow concluded that the basic needs of all humans form a hierarchy, beginning with physical, safety, belonging, and love needs, and progressing upward toward needs of esteem and self-actualization. An assumption in this model is that needs lower in the hierarchy must be met sufficiently before other needs can be addressed. Physical, safety, belonging, and love needs therefore take precedence over esteem and self-actualization needs. The goal in Maslow's model is the development of healthy people who "have sufficiently gratified their basic needs for safety, belongingness, love, respect and self-esteem so that they are intrinsically motivated . . . to strive toward self-actualization as an unceasing trend toward unity and integration within the person" (Tribe, 1982, p. 59).

What qualities and features are present in an environment designed to achieve self-actualization? Strange and Banning (2000) posited a corresponding hierarchy of environmental conditions and purposes, wherein the safety and inclusion of participants must be attended to first, followed by structures that promote involvement, and then conditions that offer full membership in a community of learning. Colleges and universities must offer safe, secure, and inclusive environments for all students. Students who lack a basic sense of belonging in an institution, free from threat, fear, and anxiety, will likely fail at other goals of learning.

The first step for campus administrators is to ensure that the physical, human aggregate, organizational, and socially constructed components of campus environments create such conditions and serve such purposes. Safety and inclusion are not the end points, though; if campus environments are to serve educational purposes, they must also engage students in significant learning experiences through meaningful and challenging roles. Without environmental structures of involvement, students risk detachment from the kinds of opportunities that call for their investment and responsibility for their own learning, key requisites for powerful educational outcomes (Astin, 1985). Finally, this model presumes that while safety, inclusion, and involvement are necessary conditions for the achievement of educational purposes, they are insufficient for ensuring an integrated whole learning experience. This requires a third level of investment—full membership in a learning community, where goals, structures, values, people, and resources come together in a seamless experience for purposes of self-actualization and fulfillment. Of particular interest is how physical, human aggregate, organizational, and constructed components on campus might detract from or contribute to the safety, inclusion, involvement, and communal experience of students with disabilities (see Figure 2.1.).

Level I: Safe and Inclusive Environments. Whether mandated by law (such as the Americans with Disabilities Act) or motivated by educational purposes, strategies to promote campus safety and inclusion involve aspects that are physical as well as psychological in nature. Freedom from physical

Figure 2.1. A Hierarchy of Learning Environments

Level III: Community
(Full Membership)

Level II: Involvement
(Participation, Engagement, Role Taking)

Level I: Safety and Inclusion
(Sense of Security and Belonging)

harm is one thing; feeling safe is another. Being physically present may meet the technical requirements of inclusion, but a sense of belonging may require another standard. Both physical and psychological aspects of the environment can detract from conditions of safety and inclusion, and either can contribute to their attainment.

Given both their functional and symbolic effects, it is obvious that the physical components of campus environments are relevant to the safety and inclusion of students with mobility, sight, and hearing disabilities. Provision of physical accessibility and accommodation is the bottom line in addressing the attraction, satisfaction, and stability of these students. Limits in either of these conditions can compromise the learning experience in fundamental ways.

Yet physical accessibility and accommodation alone do not ensure conditions for safety and inclusion for these students. Physical dimensions also convey powerful nonverbal messages. For example, the absence of an elevator may convey a lack of concern for students with mobility needs. Buildings that are hard to find or have poorly lit spaces may suggest that concerns for the safety of users have not yet been addressed (or that they are not even important). Furthermore a campus deciding to enhance physical accessibility—perhaps by molding some asphalt to the curb instead of installing proper curb cuts—might also communicate messages of "not caring enough to do it correctly," "not valuing the user," or "just responding minimally" (Strange and Banning, 2000). In contrast, a curb cut designed and constructed correctly might convey a sense that "the institution cares enough to do it right," more likely leaving an individual with mobility concerns feeling valued and appreciated.

From an aggregate perspective, safety and inclusion are also a function of congruence between the individual and the dominant human characteristics in the environment. Those who share dominant characteristics are likely to feel safe and included, while those who differ may be at risk. This "minority group paradigm" (Jones, 1996, p. 349) suggests that those in the numerical minority usually feel less welcomed on campus (whether intentionally or inadvertently) than those in the majority. Women, students of color, and persons of other than heterosexual orientation might experience this dynamic as a "chilly campus climate" (Hall and Sandler, 1982, 1984), framed by a variety of unwelcoming behaviors from others, including lack of recognition, devaluing of abilities, limited opportunities to participate, and even hostile and harassing remarks. Manifestations of exclusion may be found in discriminatory admission policies, differential distribution of financial aid, selection for academic programs, housing assignments, and various campus incidents (Hawkins, 1989). Not only does minority status present the antithesis to an inclusive environment, it also usually precludes finding sufficient role models for support (Sandeen and Rhatigan, 1990). It would be no surprise to learn that students with disabilities on a campus dominated by an able-bodied human environment might experience similar challenges.

Organizational dimensions also shape the senses of safety and inclusion of students with disabilities. Ironically, large institutions that can readily afford dedicated administrative services, such as an office of disability services, to attend to a wide range of accommodations (for example, note taking, test monitoring, recording books on tape, interpretation services) are also those where the demands for productivity and efficiency might limit the implementation of adaptive methods. In other words, the larger the scale of operation is, the more challenging it might be to respond to the labor-intensive demands of individual differences.

The power of campus culture and other socially constructed dimensions of the environment also influences perceptions of safety and inclusion. Weak social climate relationship dimensions might create an unreceptive milieu for anyone who requests special care and concern. Furthermore a homogeneous press toward fitting in might devalue individual differences, thus placing at risk (through not achieving potential or failing to succeed, for example) those whose characteristics define them as other than normal. One can imagine, for example, how an individual with a sight disability might feel on a campus where the dominant mode of communication among students is visual, such as through e-mail and chat rooms.

In sum, safe and inclusive environments are created through physical arrangements in classrooms, residence halls, campus offices, and campus grounds; human aggregate groupings (for example, theme housing); organizational structures (as in departments and campus interest groups); and social constructions (such as images, symbols, and cultural variations). Experiencing a psychological sense of belonging on campus and being free from physical threat and harm are prerequisites for the pursuit of opportunities leading to learning, growth, and development (Strange and Banning, 2000). At the very least, energy spent on coping with feelings of insecurity and exclusion can only detract from that applied to more positive growth experiences. The importance of safe and inclusive environments is that they free individuals to pursue more active engagement and higher purposes in a setting, that is, to become involved.

Level II: Involving Environments. To encourage effective learning, educational environments must go beyond ensuring the presence and security of students with disabilities. Numerous studies and reports (Astin, 1993; Chickering and Gamson, 1987; Kuh and others, 1991; Study Group on Conditions of Excellence in Higher Education, 1984) have supported the notion that learning also depends on students' active involvement in their learning environments. As a second-tier condition in this hierarchy of environmental purposes (Strange and Banning, 2000), involvement engages participants in meaningful roles and responsibilities so that each is afforded appropriate opportunities for individual growth and development. Involvement includes the investment of time and energy whereby individuals' skills are called on to contribute to the processes and outcomes of the setting (Pace, 1990).

Involving environments include physical features of human scale, flexible organizational designs, and the capacity for encouraging interaction and responding to individual needs (Strange and Banning, 2000). Are there sufficient meeting spaces? Where do students and faculty gather? How accessible are these places? What spaces isolate individuals? What spaces encourage individuals to gather? What are the traffic patterns of those who participate in the setting? Answers to these questions yield information about the involvement capacity of campus environments.

Involving environments encourage the development of campus subgroupings characterized by a commonalty of purposes and interests. Does the institution support and sustain its "community of the parts" (Spitzberg and Thorndike, 1992, p. 147)? Are campus groups given adequate resources for sustaining an ongoing agenda of educational purposes? How do students learn of the group participation options? How is participation in campus groups facilitated, recognized, and rewarded?

Involving environments offer an optimum ratio of individuals to opportunities (Chickering and Reisser, 1993; Wicker, 1984), with sufficient fixed roles and responsibilities but enough organizational flexibility to accommodate participants' individual differences of styles, abilities, and preferences. Are there sufficient opportunities for students to join and participate in leadership roles on campus? In residence halls? In student activities and organizations? In classrooms? What is the average class size? What is the ratio of faculty to students? Are resources available to cover start-up costs of new student initiatives?

Involving environments also encourage participation through cultural artifacts such as campus rituals and traditions, underscoring the availability, importance, and value of involvement (Kuh and others, 1991). What messages are communicated to prospective students about the role of campus involvement? What would a campus culture audit (Whitt, 1993) say about the value of participation and involvement in classes? In student organizations? In campus governance? What would an audit of campus cultural artifacts say? Who is excluded? Although such questions are appropriate in assessing the quality of campus involvement for all students, institutions, if they are to be successful in engaging students with disabilities, must be vigilant about how features implicated in these questions encourage or discourage these students' participation. Are meeting spaces accessible? Are images on promotion fliers appropriately inviting for all students? Are leadership role models available?

Developmentally involving environments, whether in the classroom, student organization meeting, or residence hall association, are those that exhibit characteristics of dynamic organizations, where individual differences are appreciated, participation is expected, interactions are personal rather than functional, and risk taking is encouraged (Strange, 1983). What opportunities are available for students with disabilities that sustain these conditions of involvement?

Level III: Communal Environments. Although security, inclusion, and involvement fulfill the first-tier and second-tier conditions for learning, the most powerful settings are communal (Strange and Banning, 2000). Conditions of community become evident as individuals assume significant roles over time and contribute to the very ethos and culture of the setting. Such levels of membership and involvement create a synergy of experiences in a specific time and place so as to be unique and memorable to those who have been part of the experience. Whether in the form of a student organization accomplishing special feats during a particular academic year, or a one-time, campuswide event, such as a dance marathon, involving the input and participation of numerous groups and individuals, communal environments sustain members in a bond that leaves lasting impressions in the historical and cultural evolution of a setting.

Conditions of community thrive when space is available for a group of individuals who share common characteristics and interests; when flexible organizational designs invite participation, role taking, and decision making; and when artifacts of culture extend and support community visions and purposes (Strange and Banning, 2000). These conditions compel individuals to engage one another creatively in the achievement of specific goals and outcomes. This framework, when sustained across time, is thought most powerful for the pursuit of learning (Carnegie Foundation for the Advancement of Teaching, 1990; Palmer, 1987; Strange, 1996). Where on campus do students with disabilities experience community? How are they connected to one another in community? Do they experience membership in various campus subcommunities, such as fraternities and sororities, student clubs, organizations, and advisory boards? Are they visible members of the campus community of the whole?

As implications of the electronic campus, connected to the Internet and World Wide Web, are explored and understood, it is interesting to note the potential of virtual environments for meeting a range of educational needs (Palloff and Pratt, 1999). Rapidly changing technologies offer both promises and challenges for the design and delivery of learning opportunities in postsecondary education. With appropriate access software and hardware (such as screen readers, screen enlarging programs, touch screens, and voice and alternate input devices), students with disabilities, in particular, might find the virtual community very inclusive and easier to access than negotiating the physical environment of the campus. For some forms of disability, real environments might pose significant barriers to safety, involvement, and participation. Virtual environments and other computer-mediated adaptive techniques, such as voice recognition software, might offer new levels of participation as learning environments become more flexible and accessible and are less restricted to the limits of physical space and distance. Virtual communities and real communities need not be mutually exclusive; one could enhance the sense of community in the other. In a campus environment that has an established geography or place, the virtual community could serve to strengthen rather than diminish the experience of students with disabilities (Strange and Banning, 2000). Whether real or virtual, conditions of community invoke the full capacities of students and are enriched by the unique imprint of all members, regardless of type or degree of disability.

Conclusion

A more complex and clearer understanding of the dynamics of campus environments has emerged in the literature (Baird, 1988; Conyne and Clack, 1981; Huebner and Lawson, 1990; Moos, 1979; Pascarella, 1985; Strange, 1991, 1993; Strange and Banning, 2000). The advancement of theories on the effects of educational environments has been enhanced by the presence of students who have differed in some way from the characteristics of the typical student, causing educators and researchers to reconsider the design of campus learning environments (Brookfield, 1986; Cross, 1981; Schlossberg, Lynch, and Chickering, 1989). In that respect, the influx of students with disabilities has generated new sensitivities to individual differences on campus and the need to create educational environments of ability, that is, environments capable of responding to differences. Educators committed to enhancing the experiences of students with disabilities must encourage policies, practices, and programs that secure, include, involve, and invite all students, regardless of individual differences, into the community. This requires the design and creation of environments of ability.

References

American College Personnel Association. *The Student Learning Imperative: Implications for Student Affairs.* Washington, D.C.: American College Personnel Association, 1994.
Astin, A. W. *Achieving Educational Excellence: A Critical Assessment of Priorities and Practices in Higher Education.* San Francisco: Jossey-Bass, 1985.
Astin, A. W. *What Matters in College? Four Critical Years Revisited.* San Francisco: Jossey-Bass, 1993.
Baird, L. L. "The College Environment Revisited: A Review of Research and Theory." In J. C. Smart (ed.), *Higher Education: Handbook of Theory and Research* (Vol. 4). New York: Agathon Press, 1988.

Banning, J., and Bartels, S. "A Taxonomy for Physical Artifacts: Understanding Campus Multiculturalism." *Campus Ecologist*, 1993, *11*(3), 2–3.

Brookfield, S. *Understanding and Facilitating Adult Learning.* San Francisco: Jossey-Bass, 1986.

Carnegie Foundation for the Advancement of Teaching. *Campus Life: In Search of Community.* Princeton, N.J.: Carnegie Foundation for the Advancement of Teaching, 1990.

Chickering, A. W., and Gamson, Z. F. *Principles of Good Practice for Undergraduate Education.* Racine, Wisc.: Johnson Foundation, 1987.

Chickering, A. W., and Reisser, L. *Education and Identity.* (2nd ed.) San Francisco: Jossey-Bass, 1993.

Conyne, R. K., and Clack, R. J. *Environmental Assessment and Design: A New Tool for the Applied Behavioral Scientist.* New York: Praeger, 1981.

Cross, K. P. *Adults as Learners.* San Francisco: Jossey-Bass, 1981.

Fine, M., and Asch, A. "Disability Beyond Stigma: Social Interaction, Discrimination and Activism." *Journal of Social Issues,* 1988, *44,* 3–21.

Hage, J. *Theories of Organizations: Forms, Process, and Transformation.* New York: Wiley, 1980.

Hage, J., and Aiken, M. *Social Change in Complex Organizations.* New York: Random House, 1970.

Hahn, H. "Theories and Values: Ethics and Contrasting Perspectives on Disability." In R. P. Marinelli and A. E. Dell Orto (eds.), *The Psychological and Social Impact of Disability.* (3rd ed.) New York: Springer, 1991.

Hall, R. M., and Sandler, B. R. *The Campus Climate: A Chilly One for Women: Report of the Project on the Status and Education of Women.* Washington, D.C.: Association of American Colleges, 1982.

Hall, R. M., and Sandler, B. R. *Out of the Classroom: A Chilly Campus Climate for Women: Report of the Project on the Status and Education of Women.* Washington, D.C.: Association of American Colleges, 1984.

Hawkins, B. C. "Students on Predominantly White Campuses: The Need for a New Commitment." *NASPA Journal,* 1989, *26*(3), 175–179.

Holland, J. L. *Making Vocational Choices: A Theory of Careers.* Englewood Cliffs, N.J.: Prentice Hall, 1973.

Huebner, L. A., and Lawson, J. M. "Understanding and Assessing College Environments." In D. G. Creamer and others (eds.), *College Student Development: Theory and Practice for the 1990s.* Alexandria, Va.: American College Personnel Association, 1990.

Jones, S. R. "Toward Inclusive Theory: Disability as Social Construction." *NASPA Journal,* 1996, *33,* 347–354.

Kuh, G. D., and others. *Involving Colleges: Encouraging Student Learning and Personal Development Through Out-of-Class Experiences.* San Francisco: Jossey-Bass, 1991.

Lewin, K. *Principles of Topological Psychology.* New York: McGraw-Hill, 1936.

Maslow, A. H. *Toward a Psychology of Being.* New York: Van Nostrand Reinhold, 1968.

Mehrabian, A. *Silent Messages.* (2nd ed.) Belmont, Calif.: Wadsworth, 1981.

Michelson, W. *Man and His Urban Environment: A Sociological Approach.* Reading, Mass.: Addison-Wesley, 1970.

Moos, R. H. *The Social Climate Scales: An Overview.* Palo Alto, Calif.: Consulting Psychologists Press, 1968.

Moos, R. H. *Evaluating Educational Environments.* San Francisco: Jossey-Bass, 1979.

Moos, R. H. *The Human Context: Environmental Determinants of Behavior.* Malabar, Fla.: Robert E. Krieger, 1986.

Moos, R. H., and Trickett, E. J. *Classroom Environment Scale Manual.* Palo Alto, Calif.: Consulting Psychologists Press, 1974.

Pace, C. *The Undergraduates: A Report of Their Activities and Progress in College in the 1980s.* Los Angeles: Center for the Study of Evaluation, University of California, 1990.

Palloff, R. M., and Pratt, K. *Building Learning Communities in Cyberspace: Effective Strategies for the Online Classroom.* San Francisco: Jossey-Bass, 1999.

Palmer, P. J. "Community, Conflict, and Ways of Knowing." *Change,* 1987, *19*(5), 20–25.

Pascarella, E. T. "College Environmental Influences on Learning and Cognitive Development: A Critical Review and Synthesis." In J. C. Smart (ed.), *Higher Education: Handbook of Theory and Research* (Vol. 1). New York: Agathon Press, 1985.

Price, J. L. *Handbook of Organizational Measurement.* Lexington, Mass.: Heath, 1972.

Sandeen, A., and Rhatigan, J. J. "New Pressures for Social Responsiveness and Accountability." In M. J. Barr and M. L. Upcraft (eds.), *New Futures for Student Affairs.* San Francisco: Jossey-Bass, 1990.

Schein, E. H. *Organizational Culture and Leadership.* (2nd ed.) San Francisco: Jossey-Bass, 1992.

Schlossberg, N., Lynch, A. Q., and Chickering, A. W. *Improving Higher Education Environments for Adults: Responsive Programs and Services from Entry to Departure.* San Francisco: Jossey-Bass, 1989.

Smart, J. C., Feldman, K. A., and Ethington, C. A. *Academic Disciplines: Holland's Theory and the Study of College Students and Faculty.* Nashville, Tenn.: Vanderbilt University Press, 2000.

Spitzberg, I. J., Jr., and Thorndike, V. V. *Creating Community on College Campuses.* Albany: State University of New York Press, 1992.

Stern, G. *People in Context: Measuring Person-Environment Congruence in Education and Industry.* New York: Wiley, 1970.

Stern, R. A. *Pride of Place: Building the American Dream.* Boston: Houghton Mifflin, 1986.

Strange, C. C. "Human Development Theory and Administrative Practice in Student Affairs: Ships Passing in the Daylight?" *NASPA Journal,* 1983, *21,* 2–8.

Strange, C. C. "Managing College Environments: Theory and Practice." In T. K. Miller and others, *Administration and Leadership in Student Affairs: Actualizing Student Development in Student Affairs.* (2nd ed.) Muncie, Ind.: Accelerated Development, 1991.

Strange, C. C. "Theories and Concepts of Campus Living Environments." In R. B. Winston, Jr., and others (eds.), *Student Housing and Residential Life: A Handbook for the Professional Committed to Student Development Goals.* San Francisco: Jossey-Bass, 1993.

Strange, C. C. "Dynamics of Campus Environments." In S. R. Komives and D. B. Woodard (eds.), *Student Services: A Handbook for the Profession.* (3rd ed.) San Francisco: Jossey-Bass, 1996.

Strange, C. C., and Banning, J. *Educating by Design: Creating Campus Environments That Work.* San Francisco: Jossey-Bass, 2000.

Study Group on Conditions of Excellence in Higher Education. *Involvement in Learning: Realizing the Potential of American Higher Education.* Washington, D.C.: National Institute of Education, 1984.

Sturner, W. F. "The College Environment." In D. W. Vermilye (ed.), *The Future in the Making.* San Francisco: Jossey-Bass, 1973.

Thelin, J. R., and Yankovich, J. "Bricks and Mortar: Architecture and the Study of Higher Education." In J. C. Smart (ed.), *Higher Education: Handbook of Theory and Research* (Vol. 3). New York: Agathon Press, 1987.

Tribe, C. *Profile of Three Theories: Erikson, Maslow, Piaget.* Dubuque, Iowa: Kendall/Hunt, 1982.

Whitt, E. J. "Making the Familiar Strange: Discovering Culture." In G. D. Kuh (ed.), *Using Cultural Perspectives in Student Affairs.* Alexandria, Va.: ACPA Media, 1993.

Wicker, A. *An Introduction to Ecological Psychology.* New York: Cambridge University Press, 1984.

CARNEY STRANGE *is professor of higher education and student affairs, Bowling Green State University in Bowling Green, Ohio.*

3

This chapter examines the issues that can affect the recruitment and admission of students with disabilities and provides suggestions to student affairs professionals for ensuring their active participation in the recruitment and admission process.

Recruitment and Admission of Students with Disabilities

Barbara J. Palombi

Many individuals with disabilities want opportunities similar to those of their nondisabled peers, including a college education, work, and a successful life. College and postsecondary vocational programs are positively related to employment and success for both disabled and nondisabled individuals (Fairweather and Shaver, 1990). With the passage of Section 504 of the Rehabilitation Act of 1973, students who had not previously aspired to higher education found that colleges and universities were more responsive to their needs than before. In 1975, The Education of All Handicapped Children Act (Public Law 94-142) was passed by the U.S. Congress (Leyser, Vogel, and Wyland, 1998). This legislation "mandated that all individuals with disabilities receive an appropriate education and resulted in a significantly larger number of students with disabilities identified and served in elementary and secondary schools" (Leyser, Vogel, and Wyland, 1998, p. 5). As a result of the efforts by administrators of elementary and secondary schools, individuals with disabilities became aware of their postsecondary options. As a consequence of the removal of significant barriers, the number of students with disabilities in higher education dramatically increased in the 1980s (Leyser, Vogel, and Wyland, 1998).

In Chapter One of this volume, Hall and Belch provided evidence of the significant increase in enrollment of students with disabilities over the past twenty-five years. Leyser, Vogel, and Wyland (1998) have contended that the most noticeable increase in college enrollment between 1988 and 1994 among students with disabilities was students with learning disabilities. Yet little is known about the participation of youths with disabilities in postsecondary education. Previous research has been piecemeal, focusing

NEW DIRECTIONS FOR STUDENT SERVICES, no. 91, Fall 2000 © Jossey-Bass Publishers on either a geographical area or on youths with a specific type of disability (Fairweather and Shaver, 1990). Much of the current educational and psychological literature concerning students with disabilities looks at students with learning disabilities. This chapter examines the recruitment and admissions of students with disabilities and the issues that arise due to the special needs of this population.

Recruitment Process

A study conducted by the National Longitudinal Transition Study of Special Education Students (National Transition Study) followed secondary-level special education students from high school to early adulthood (Fairweather and Shaver, 1990). The researchers found that participation for disabled youths in both two-year and four-year colleges was well below the national average for nondisabled youths and socially and economically disadvantaged youths (Fairweather and Shaver, 1990). The reasons cited for this discrepancy were a lack of effective training and education in secondary school, inaccessibility to college preparatory programs, weak linkages between secondary and postsecondary educational institutions, and a lack of transition-oriented programs for youths with disabilities (Fairweather and Shaver, 1990).

For students with disabilities, the type of postsecondary institution— vocational, two-year, or four-year—they received information from through institutional visitations or contact with institutional representatives directly influenced their selection for attendance (Miller, Rzonca, and Snider, 1991). These data support the need for a stronger linkage between high schools and four-year colleges (Fairweather and Shaver, 1990).

In order for four-year institutions to attract students with disabilities, representatives from these institutions might need to ensure that students with disabilities have sufficient information about four-year institutions through staff visitations to high schools and speaking to students with disabilities, arranging on-campus visits that focus on services available to students with disabilities, or targeting literature distributions to high school students with disabilities. Representatives need to be able to articulate the type and extent of special services that are available at their respective institutions. For example, if a prospective student with a disability approaches an admissions staff member and inquires about support services and accommodations, the staff member might simply provide the student with contact information for the office and staff member for students with disabilities and expect the prospective student to secure the relevant information. The student might interpret the limited information or the offer of contact information as a lack of interest and therefore no longer consider the institution. The type and extensiveness of available support services are important to students with a disability in determining the selection of a college or university (Kavale and Forness, 1996). Students with disabilities who are trying to determine the support services available in colleges and universities must conduct extensive research in order to gain an understanding and knowledge of "1) how to read and evaluate the many guides available; 2) how to locate services in colleges not listed in the guide; and 3) how to evaluate the located services" (Cowen, 1993, p. 40). It is important for admissions and student affairs staff members to be well versed in the services and accommodations provided at the institution they represent.

The successful inclusion of students with disabilities in postsecondary education requires a comprehensive and programmatic approach (Siperstein, 1988). In the past, colleges and universities have designed outreach programs to increase the number of historically underrepresented students in higher education (women, ethnic and racial minorities, first-generation students) to encourage their enrollment and assist in their transition from high school to college. Similar strategies might serve as a framework for designing programs for students with disabilities.

Boston College has organized a five-day campus-based program that provides high school students with disabilities an opportunity to preview college life. Entitled "A Taste of College," this program affords high school juniors and seniors with learning disabilities opportunities to meet with professors, attend college lectures, learn self-advocacy skills, and stay in a residence hall. Workshops on time management, note-taking skills, and test preparation are offered as part of the program as well (Brinckerhoff, 1996).

A program such as the Hispanic Mother-Daughter Program entitled "Second Generation" at Arizona State University (1994) can serve as a model for institutions to emulate in recruiting students with disabilities. This program has been effective in helping to educate parents and enlist their support in preparing their daughters to obtain a college education. A program of this nature could be adapted to help students with disabilities who aspire to a college education and subsequently enroll. For example, a similar program might assist parents in identifying the differences in legal mandates and provide them with appropriate information to ensure that their son or daughter is enrolled in college preparatory classes, completes assignments similar to those required in college, reads textbooks effectively, knows how to study and organize study time and space, functions independently, develops written language skills, and learns how to take standardized tests such as the Scholastic Aptitude Test (SAT) or American College Test (ACT) (Mangrum and Strichart, 1988; Scott, 1991). Without this information, parents might assume that their child's high school experience provides sufficient preparation for college and then find this was not the case when their son or daughter is denied admission.

The recruitment process is the first step in ensuring that students with disabilities consider enrolling in two-year and four-year institutions of higher education. Student affairs staff members might assist these students in bridging the gap between high school and postsecondary institutions. These staff members have the educational and experiential background and skills needed to develop interventions that could achieve this objective and help students, parents, and high school personnel develop an awareness of institutions and the type of support services available. The next step for students with disabilities in gaining access to institutions of higher education is having an admission process that deals with their special issues.

Admissions Process

The process of applying, being admitted to, and matriculating in an institution of postsecondary education can be complicated and arduous for all students, and especially for students with disabilities. Many students with disabilities move from an environment in which school personnel have identified their needs and provided appropriate services under Public Law 94-142 to an environment in which students themselves are expected to provide documentation of their disability and request specific accommodations (Brinckerhoff, 1996; Fairweather and Shaver, 1990; HEATH, 2000; Scott, 1991). Issues regarding confidentiality and disclosure of disability, the use of standardized test scores in making admission decisions, and requesting accommodations are significant to students with disabilities in the application and admission process.

Section 504 of the Rehabilitation Act of 1973 and the Americans with Disabilities Act of 1990 (ADA) prohibit any preadmission inquiry regarding a student's disability (White, 1998). A representative of the Office of Civil Rights (OCR) of the U.S. Department of Education stated that "a high school counselor might honestly communicate the contents of a student's curriculum, which may imply a learning, or other, disability, but may not disclose or discuss the disability itself without parental consent" (White, 1998, p. 8). Because of the limits placed on the high school counselors, a greater degree of responsibility is placed on the student to inform a college or university regarding his or her disability (White, 1998).

Disclosure of disability, or self-identification as disabled, is a significant issue in the admission process. Early in this process, students with disabilities are faced with a decision of whether to request appropriate accommodation in taking any standardized test required for admission. The Educational Testing Service has provided a number of accommodations (there are large-print version, extra test time, readers, cassette versions, and special equipment) to students who identify themselves as having a disability and provide appropriate documentation (Belch, 1995). The test results carry a notation indicating "nonstandardized" testing administration. Indeed, "the key issue for applicants in availing themselves of these particular accommodations during the testing procedure is that they relinquish confidentiality of disability by virtue of the non-standardized notation on the score reports that are submitted to the institution" (Belch, 1995, p. 104). The alternative for a student with a disability is not to request accommodation during testing, with the risk of scoring poorly. In either case, poor test scores or the report of a nonstandardized test score might be viewed as a marker by staff making admission decisions (Belch, 1995). The dilemma for students with disabilities is that they cannot receive accommodation in the testing process and maintain confidentiality in the preadmission process.

A degree of flexibility regarding particular qualifications does exist for admissions personnel (HEATH, 2000; Kirst, 1999). For example, some institutions might use written essays, leadership abilities, work experience, community service, low-income, or a single-parent home as part of their admission criteria (Kirst, 1999). As a result, HEATH (2000) suggested that high school students with disabilities consider the option of disclosing their disability during the application process. Disclosure provides the applicant with an opportunity to explain any discrepancies in admission documents (HEATH, 2000). For example, a student with a learning disability might have a discrepancy between excellent high school grades and low standardized test scores. Explaining such disparities does not guarantee admission but does allow students to provide relevant information to admission staff to use in the decision-making process.

Regardless of whether a student voluntarily chooses to disclose the disability, standardized test scores have been used as one of the means to evaluate an applicant's suitability for admission. For applicants with disabilities, however, use of standardized test scores could have adverse effects on admission. Some standardized tests discriminate against students with disabilities (Jarrow, 1992; Rothstein, 1991). Students with learning disabilities and hearing impairments, for example, perform well below the general admissions test-taking population in postsecondary admission tests (Bennett and Ragosta, 1985). The two best predictors of success for students with learning disabilities have been identified as the number of regular high school English courses completed with a grade of C or better and overall grade point average (GPA) (Vogel and Adelman, 1992). Consistent with recommendations for applicants without disabilities, admissions officers should weigh high school preparation and performance (as reflected in high school courses and GPA) more heavily than admission test scores for students with disabilities (Vogel and Adelman, 1992).

In a study of 502 postsecondary institutions concerning admission procedures for students with disabilities, approximately half of the postsecondary institutions surveyed do not modify admissions procedures or standards for students with disabilities who disclose in the admissions process (Vogel and others, 1998). However, research-oriented postsecondary institutions most often used an additional review process involving a knowledgeable staff or faculty member in reviewing the application materials. Twenty-one percent of the institutions surveyed "used the standard admissions procedures, asked a knowledgeable staff or faculty member to review the application materials, and also modified the admissions standards, by making them less stringent for students who disclosed a disability" (Vogel and others, 1998, p. 239).

In acknowledgment of existing evidence, the American Association of Collegiate Registrars and Admissions Officers (AACRAO) recommended that institutions of higher education not rely solely on objective criteria (such as GPAs and standardized test scores) in admission decisions for students with disabilities (Douvanis, 1998; Spillane, McGuire, and Norlander, 1992). Less emphasis on standardized test scores may be an acknowledgment that their usefulness in predicting the academic performance of students with disabilities has yet to be determined. In any case, institutions need to make explicit the academic (for example, GPA and test scores) and nonacademic (for example, the personal interview, letters of recommendation, and a personal statement) criteria they use to determine which applicants with disabilities are admitted to their institutions.

Some critics of the admission policies that institutions of higher education use believe that the institutions need to be more accommodating to students with disabilities and offer alternative course or academic requirements, reduce academic course loads, and make similar accommodations that are required or mandated by Public Law 94-142 (Brinckerhoff, Shaw, and McGuire, 1992; Stolowitz, 1995). Section 504 does not require institutions that have selection criteria to lower their admission standards; however, it does require them to apply those standards equally to all applicants, with or without disabilities (Spillane, McGuire, and Norlander, 1992).

Application forms cannot require applicants to disclose a disability; however, the information can be requested after admission on a voluntary basis (Diminnie, 1992). A college or university with a history of past discrimination regarding students with disabilities or a desire to encourage participation by students with disabilities might ask applicants for admission to self-identify on the application form (HEATH, 2000). Should a student decide to disclose his or her disability, this information cannot be used to deny admission (HEATH, 2000).

To ensure that students with disabilities are considered in a manner consistent with their nondisabled peers, admissions and student affairs professionals must develop and implement written policies and procedures concerning admission, diagnosis, accommodation, curriculum requirements, and service delivery to students with disabilities (National Joint Committee on Learning Disabilities, 1996). The AACRAO guidelines "recognize the need for advisory committees to assist in developing admission policies, practices, and procedures that comply with the letter and spirit of Section 504 and the ADA" (Spillane, McGuire, and Norlander, 1992, p. 669). To determine if these policies and procedures do not discriminate illegally, admissions and student affairs professionals should review the rate of acceptance and rejection for applicants with disabilities and compare them to the rate of admission for their nondisabled peers. Differences in these rates might or might not demonstrate discrimination but would provide important information for further examination. Full implementation of Section 504 requires that each postsecondary institution receiving federal funds conduct periodic validity studies correlating the predictors used not only with first-year grades but also with the attainment of the college degree for students with disabilities (Spillane, McGuire, and Norlander, 1992).

Another possible consideration for university personnel and students with disabilities is to simplify the college application process. A recent trend for all students is the use of the Common Application form and the College Link program (Rubenstone and Dalby, 1994). For a fee, applicants complete a single application on their personal computer and can forward that application to approximately five hundred participating institutions. Students provide their guidance counselor with their application on diskette; then the guidance counselor forwards all transcripts, recommendations, and the application to member institutions.

Students with disabilities might also need information concerning the various components of the admission process (recommendations, written essays, interviews, and so forth). A preadmission workshop offered by student affairs staff members might assist students with disabilities in gaining that information. For example, if an essay is required for admission, providing some examples of well-written essays might help students with disabilities understand the expectations of that part of the application. If references are needed, who might serve as good references? If the SAT or ACT is required, suggest that the student apply for testing accommodations so that the limitations of the disability do not detract from the student's intellectual ability. These minor accommodations might help clarify the application process and encourage students with disabilities to apply to institutions of higher education.

It is appropriate to encourage students who may need accommodations to declare those as soon as possible after notification of admission. Service provider contact information should be provided in the application packet. Admissions staff members need to establish strong relationships with staff who serve students with disabilities in order to obtain the necessary information and counsel from them regarding self-identification. Accommodation requests should remain separate and distinct from the admission review process (Belch, 1995; Harris, Horn, and McCarthy, 1994). A distinct procedure should exist that instructs students who are notified of admission whom to contact and how to request appropriate accommodations.

Conclusion

The knowledge and awareness of admission staff, the use of academic and nonacademic criteria in admission decisions, and confidentiality in the process are crucial issues for student affairs professionals to consider in the recruitment and admission process for students with disabilities. In order to recruit qualified students with disabilities, every admission staff member needs to be aware of the type and extent of services available at their respective institutions. Many offices for students with disabilities are located within the division of student affairs. This places the responsibility of educating admission staff members as to the type and extent of support services available at their institution with student affair professionals.

Admission decisions for students with disabilities cannot be based solely on standardized test scores. Nonacademic criteria, in conjunction with academic criteria, need to be considered on an individual basis for qualified applicants with disabilities based on the type of disability.

The lack of confidentiality in the admission process for students with disabilities is a concern. Confidentiality is closely guarded for other students, yet students with disabilities are caught in a position of relinquishing confidentiality in order to secure needed accommodations for testing or to explain discrepancies in academic records.

The core values of the student affairs profession of community, equality, and human dignity that Hall and Belch (see Chapter One) have discussed must be reflected in the procedures and policies associated with the admission process. Student affairs professionals need to ensure that all students, including students with disabilities, who have any contact with their institution are dealt with in a manner that reflects these values.

These areas of concern provide a complex and challenging task for student affairs professionals. Addressing these issues will ensure that students with disabilities will have an equal opportunity to be recruited and admitted to institutions of higher education.

References

Arizona State University. *Second Generation.* Tempe: Office of Student Life, Arizona State University, 1994.

Belch, H. A. "Admitting Graduate Students with Disabilities." In A. S. Pruitt and P. D. Isaac (eds.), *Student Services for the Changing Graduate Student Population.* New Directions for Student Services, no. 72. San Francisco: Jossey-Bass, 1995.

Bennett, R. E., and Ragosta, M. "Technical Characteristics of Postsecondary Admissions Test for Handicapped Examinees: A Review of Research." *Journal of Special Education,* 1985, *19*(3), 255–267.

Brinckerhoff, L. C. "Making the Transition to Higher Education: Opportunities for Student Empowerment." *Journal of Learning Disabilities,* 1996, *29*(2), 18–35.

Brinckerhoff, L. C., Shaw, S. F., and McGuire, J. M. "Promoting Access, Accommodations, and Independence for College Students with Learning Disabilities." *Journal of Learning Disabilities,* 1992, *25*(7), 418–429.

Cowen, S. "Transition Planning for Learning Disabled College-Bound Students." In S. A. Vogel and P. B. Adelman (eds.), *Success for College Students with Learning Disabilities.* New York: Springer-Verlag, 1993.

Diminnie, C. B. *An Essential Guide to Graduate Admissions.* Washington, D.C.: Council of Graduate Schools, 1992. (ED 354 844)

Douvanis, G. "After Hopwood: Weighing the Legal Implications for College Admissions." *College Board Review,* 1998, *184,* 6–11.

Fairweather, J. S., and Shaver, D. M. "A Troubled Future? Participation in Postsecondary Education by Youths with Disabilities." *Journal of Higher Education,* 1990, *61*(3), 332–348.

Harris, R. W., Horn, C. A., and McCarthy, M. A. "Physical and Technological Access." In D. Ryan and M. A. McCarthy (eds.), *A Student Affairs Guide to the Americans with Disabilities Act and Disability Issues.* Washington, D.C.: National Association of Student Personnel Administrators, 1994.

HEATH. *Getting Ready for College: Advising High School Students with Learning Disabilities.* Washington, D.C.: American Council on Education, HEATH Resource Center, 2000. [http://www.kidsource.com/Heath/gr.html].

Jarrow, J. *Title by Title: The Americans with Disabilities Act's Impact on Postsecondary Education.* Columbus, Ohio: Association on Higher Education and Disability, 1992.

Kavale, K. A., and Forness, S. R. "Learning Disability Grows Up: Rehabilitation Issues for Individuals with Learning Disabilities." *Journal of Rehabilitation,* Jan.–Mar. 1996, pp. 34–41.

Kirst, M. W. *New Criteria for College Admissions.* [http://www.edweek.org/ew/1999 /32kirst.h18]. 1999.

Leyser, Y., Vogel, S., and Wyland, S. "Faculty Attitudes and Practice Regarding Students with Disabilities: Two Decades After Implementation of Section 504." *Journal of Postsecondary Education and Disability,* 1998, *13*(3), 5–19.

Mangrum, C. T., and Strichart, S. S. *College and the Learning Disabled Student.* (2nd ed.) Philadelphia: Grune & Stratton, 1988.

Miller, R. J., Rzonca, C., and Snider, B. "Variables Related to the Type of Postsecondary Education Experience Chosen by Young Adults with Learning Disabilities." *Journal of Learning Disabilities,* 1991, *24*(3), 188–191.

National Joint Committee on Learning Disabilities. "Secondary to Postsecondary Education Transition Planning for Students with Learning Disabilities." *Learning Disability Quarterly,* 1996, *19,* 62–63.

Rothstein, L. F. "Students, Staff, and Faculty with Disabilities: Current Issues for Colleges and Universities." *Journal of College and University Law,* 1991, *17*(4), 471–482.

Rubenstone, S., and Dalby, S. *College Admissions: A Crash Course for Panicked Parents.* New York: Macmillan, 1994.

Scott, S. S. "A Change in Legal Status: An Overlooked Dimension in the Transition to Higher Education." *Journal of Learning Disabilities,* 1991, *24*(8), 459–466.

Siperstein, G. N. "Students with Learning Disabilities in College: The Need for a Programmatic Approach to Critical Transitions." *Journal of Learning Disabilities,* 1988, *21*(7), 431–435.

Spillane, S. A., McGuire, J. M., and Norlander, K. A. "Undergraduate Admission Policies, Practices, and Procedures for Applicants with Learning Disabilities." *Journal of Learning Disabilities,* 1992, *25*(10), 665–677.

Stolowitz, M. A. "How to Achieve Academic and Creative Success in Spite of the Inflexible, Unresponsive Higher Education System." *Journal of Learning Disabilities,* 1995, *28*(1), 4–6.

Vogel, S. A., and Adelman, P. B. "The Success of College Students with Learning Disabilities: Factors Related to Educational Attainment." *Journal of Learning Disabilities,* 1992, *25*(7), 430–441.

Vogel, S. A., and others. "The National Learning Disabilities Postsecondary Data Bank: An Overview." *Journal of Learning Disabilities,* 1998, *31*(3), 234–247.

White, S. "Disclosure and College Admission." *Journal of College Admission,* 1998, *161*(7), 5–11.

BARBARA J. PALOMBI *is director of training, Career Planning and Counseling Center, at Grand Valley State University in Allendale, Michigan.*

4

Targeting internships; service learning; study abroad; and sports, recreation, and intramural sports can enhance campus life for college students with disabilities.

Enhancing Out-of-Class Opportunities for Students with Disabilities

Donna Johnson

Involvement in out-of-class activities has been identified as a critical element in contributing positively to student outcomes, among them, persistence, cognitive and intellectual development, interpersonal and intrapersonal competence, practical competence, and subsequent postgraduation success (Astin, 1993; Kuh, 1995; Kuh, Branch Douglas, Lund, and Ramin-Gyurnek, 1994; Kuh and others, 1991; Pace, 1990; Pascarella and Terenzini, 1991). Although research indicates that no single variable explains persistence, Astin (1993) found that prior academic achievement, college academic performance, living on campus, and involvement in out-of-class activities all contribute significantly to persistence. Research studies have concluded that involvement in clubs and organizations, student-faculty interaction, a balance between academic and social involvement, interaction with diverse peers, and environments distinguishable by nondiscriminatory attitudes contribute to cognitive and intellectual development—for example, critical thinking, reasoning, complex meaning making, and comprehension (Astin, 1993; Kuh, 1995; Kuh, Branch Douglas, Lund, and Ramin-Gyurnek, 1994; Pascarella and Terenzini, 1991). Positive outcomes related to interpersonal and intrapersonal competence, such as identity, self-confidence, and the ability to relate to others, are associated with leadership roles, involvement in student organizations, study-abroad experiences, and interacting with peers who have diverse perspectives (Astin, 1993; Kuh, 1995; Kuh, Branch Douglas, Lund, and Ramin-Gyurnek, 1994; Pascarella and Terenzini, 1991). Similar experiences such as leadership roles, interactions with faculty, and involvement in student organizations all contribute to gains in practical competence, such as career decision making and independent action (Astin,

1993; Kuh, Branch Douglas, Lund, and Ramin-Gyurnek, 1994; Pascarella and Terenzini, 1991).

Kuh and others (1991) reported that out-of-class experiences increase students' satisfaction with college, promote leadership development, and enhance opportunities for career success. Schuh and Laverty (1983) found that participation in out-of-class activities builds teamwork and decision-making and planning skills, which in turn promote postgraduate managerial skills. In a 1989 study, Erwin postulated that participation in recreation programs may advance students' self-determination and ethical development and increase students' ability to get along with others. Recreation programs build students' decision-making abilities (Dattilo and Murphy, 1987) and result in increased feelings of wellness, reduced stress levels, greater regard for others, and increased self-esteem (Bryant, Banta, and Bradley, 1995). Similar benefits to students who participated in outdoor recreation programs include positive changes "in self-concept, self-esteem, trust, group cooperation, skill development, improved health and more" (Anderson and others, 1997, p. 215).

In a 1990 study, the Carnegie Foundation for the Advancement of Teaching reported that out-of-class experiences are important for the following reasons: a large portion of students' time is spent outside the classroom, how students spend their free time is dependent on their peer group, and through participation in out-of-class activities, students develop skills they are not likely to develop in the classroom. The amount of time and energy that students devote to involvement in campus activities, as well as the level of responsibility or engagement (in organizing, planning, and implementing) provided, serve to enhance the learning experience (Astin, 1993; Pace, 1990).

Educational goals and learning outcomes are important for all students in postsecondary education, including students with disabilities. Issues of persistence, interpersonal and intrapersonal competence, practical competence, and postgraduation success are particularly salient for students with disabilities. Only half of enrolled students with disabilities earned a degree compared to two-thirds of their nondisabled peers (National Center for Education Statistics, 1999). Students with disabilities represent a higher proportion of unemployed college graduates (National Center for Education Statistics, 1999). A national survey of first-year students in 1998 revealed that students with disabilities self-reported lower rankings than their nondisabled counterparts on measures of self-esteem, academic ability, and physical strength (Henderson, 1999). Participation in sports and recreation provides students with disabilities the opportunity to develop social relationships, build self-esteem, and improve physical strength and stamina (Hedrick and Broadbent, 1996).

Section 504 of the Rehabilitation Act of 1973 and the 1990 Americans with Disabilities Act (ADA) require colleges and universities to provide access and reasonable academic accommodations (such as note takers and additional time on exams). Despite the required programmatic access as outlined in Section 504, accommodations in out-of-class activities have been a secondary priority for many campuses. Compliance with the legislation has historically focused on removing architectural barriers, with less attention given to attitudinal barriers and programmatic access (Jarrow, 1993).

In response to the need for greater emphasis on programmatic access and dispelling attitudinal barriers, disability service providers must explore ways in which to enhance out-of-class experiences for college students with disabilities. This chapter focuses on ways to improve the involvement of students with disabilities with campus life activities, experiential learning (internships and service learning), study abroad, and sports and recreation.

Campus Life Activities

Because many out-of-class activities build leadership skills, students with disabilities should be able to participate in these activities. Campus life and disability service staff must work together to ensure equal access to out-of-class activities for students with disabilities. For example, campus life staff should view disability as a part of overall student diversity and see accommodating students with disabilities as welcoming another historically underrepresented group to campus. Staff who provide service to students with disabilities should view arranging academic accommodations as only part of this job; they need to collaborate with other campus professionals to ensure that these students feel as encouraged to and have an equal opportunity to participate in out-of-class activities as their nondisabled peers.

Strategies for Encouraging Participation. Student affairs professionals and faculty must understand their legal obligations regarding student participation in out-of-class activities. Under Title II of the ADA, students with disabilities have the right to participate in programs or activities that are available to people without disabilities. This means that if the institution sponsors field trips, leadership retreats, or homecoming festivities, these activities must be available to students with disabilities. Transportation to and the physical location of an event are items that need attention and consideration as a matter of course in the planning process. The inclusion of a care attendant or interpreter should be accounted for or discussed in the planning stages in order to anticipate a possibility that exists rather than react to a request by a specific student. One way to communicate an expectation of participation is to include disability access statements on all promotional materials. The statement, "Disability accommodations available upon request," can indicate a welcoming and inclusive environment, essential to creating a productive learning environment (Strange and Banning, 2000).

One way to determine the accessibility—physical, programmatic, informational, and attitudinal—of campus life activities is an access initiative, which is a tangible plan that directs staff in translating new knowledge into action by clarifying goals and objectives, identifying resources, assigning individual responsibility, and developing a measurement of progress (Chelberg, Harbour, and Juarez, 1998). Campus life staff should also complete a needs assessment to identify major barriers to participation for students with disabilities.

Examples of Inclusiveness. Ball State University has a long history of creating an inclusive environment on campus for students, faculty, and staff with disabilities. A guiding philosophy of providing access and opportunities is complemented by the collaborative nature in which planning and implementation occur (Vickery and McClure, 1998). Over time, Ball State University officials have elevated the meaning and nature of access to activities and programs on campus. Shared decision making, interdisciplinary committees, and pooled financial resources are the means to sustain commitment to providing meaningful access and full participation to students with disabilities on campus (Vickery and McClure, 1998).

At Ball State University, initial efforts in the 1960s of providing structural changes (such as curb cuts) to assist students with mobility impairments served as a precursor for ongoing efforts, including the campuswide availability of telecommunication devices for the deaf (TDDs), installation of an infrared sound system in the performing arts auditorium, and the availability of FM listening systems to enrich the experience for individuals with hearing loss (Vickery and McClure, 1998). In addition, videos available in the campus library have been enhanced with audio description and captioning benefiting students with visual impairments or learning disabilities. Braille and large-print production is utilized for preadmission visits, and job postings are provided in electronic media from Career Services (Vickery and McClure, 1998).

As Temple University embarked on several new building projects, Disability Resources and Services staff and disability-related community and university groups participated in the planning stages to integrate disability-friendly aspects within overall building design (D. Cebula, personal communication, Sept. 30, 1999). Two new residence halls were designed with several options for disability-friendly rooms and suites. A large state-of-the-art recreation and fitness center was designed with adaptive equipment, including a three-station Para-gym, a Buggy Roller treadmill, a Power Trainer, and a custom table for free weight exercises. Students who use racing chairs for additional fitness conditioning have used the indoor jogging track.

Internships and Service Learning

College graduates with disabilities experience higher unemployment rates and longer job searches, and they are more likely to be employed outside their chosen field than graduates without disabilities (Frank, Karst, and Boles, 1989). In addition, although the ADA was passed a decade ago, students with disabilities still are unsure about their employment rights under it, particularly regarding disclosure of disabilities (Aune and Kroeger, 1997;

Thompson and Dooley-Dickey, 1994). In another study, Hitchings and others (1998) reported that less than 20 percent of the students with disabilities surveyed were able to explain how their disability would affect them in carrying out job responsibilities.

Structured experiences, such as internships and service learning, provide opportunities for students to develop a wide range of skills and knowledge. Participation in internships promotes job skills and enhances grade point average (Astin, 1993). Students with disabilities can benefit from experiential learning opportunities because they offer ways to develop academic, career, and personal growth skills (Laycock, Hermon, and Laetz, 1992; Trach and Harney, 1998). Work and field experiences also enrich classroom learning through practical application in the workplace (Stern, Hopkins, McMillion, and Cagampang, 1992), and many employers tend to hire their interns as permanent full-time employees (Lindquist, 1993).

Strategies for Encouraging Participation. Because experiential learning offers an ideal means for students to gain marketable skills and address disability issues in the work setting, experiential learning coordinators and disability service providers must actively recruit students with disabilities to participate in these programs. Disclosure statements expressing that disability accommodations are available on request should be placed in all brochures, posters, and Web sites advertising internship and service-learning opportunities. Information sessions that include panels of professionals should include individuals with disabilities who can serve as role models in the workforce.

Experiential learning staff also must understand students' rights and responsibilities under the ADA. Under Title II, students with disabilities have the right to participate in programs or activities that are available to people without disabilities. This means that if the institution sponsors internships and service-learning opportunities for students, it must make these opportunities available to students with disabilities. Internship and service-learning staff should also receive training on disability issues, such as creating welcoming environments and using appropriate disability language.

Experiential learning opportunities serve as practical situations, where students can learn and make mistakes. They also provide opportunities for students to practice advocating for themselves with regard to workplace accommodation issues. For example, students can test workplace accommodations (such as adapted keyboards, magnification systems that enlarge text, computer-aided transcription, and earplugs to remove excessive distractions) in a relatively low-risk environment and reflect on whether, when, and how to disclose their disability at the experiential learning sites.

Experiential learning coordinators and disability service providers should collaborate to identify accessible internship and service-learning opportunities and assist students in identifying their options. One way of doing this is by conducting accessibility surveys of organizations that post internships and service-learning opportunities on campus. Surveys should address the physical, programmatic, informational, and attitudinal accessibility of the organization and its ability to accommodate experiential learners with disabilities (Chelberg, Harbour, and Juarez, 1998). Disability services providers should be available to provide technical assistance to help organizations make access improvements. In addition, information on companies with a history of employing individuals with a disability, such as IBM and Marriott, should be available, and efforts should be made to contact these companies for internship opportunities.

Examples of Inclusiveness. The University of Washington developed the DO-IT CAREERS (Careers, Academics, Research, Experiential Education and Relevant Skills) project in 1997 with funding from the U.S. Department of Education, Office of Special Education and Rehabilitative Services, Office of Special Education Programs. The project's purpose was to increase the participation of college students with disabilities in work experiences that will help them build career skills (J. Smallman, personal communication, Sept. 30, 1999). The goal for each DO-IT participant is not simply job placement, but the pursuit of a meaningful career that matches the student's goals, interests, and abilities.

The project seeks to increase the knowledge and understanding of students with disabilities, career development professionals and employers about the legal rights, accommodation needs, and capabilities of employees and interns with disabilities (J. Smallman, personal communication, Sept. 30, 1999). This is accomplished through printed materials and videotapes, electronic mentoring discussion groups, conference and community presentations, and individual consultation. In three years, DO-IT CAREERS staff has provided information to more than 800 students with disabilities, 900 career development professionals, and 150 employers.

Study Abroad

Although studying abroad is one of the most effective ways to prepare college graduates to contribute to an increasingly global and interdependent society (Kauffmann, Martin, and Weaver, 1992), most colleges and universities lack a consistent process for recruiting and advising students with disabilities for study abroad and often have insufficient knowledge about the accessibility of study sites for these students. Students with disabilities are therefore not encouraged to study abroad.

A 1990 survey of ninety-nine international exchange programs by Mobility International found that 54 percent had never had a participant with a disability (Bucks, 1997). In a survey of Big Ten institutions, students with disabilities were less than 1 percent of students who studied abroad (Aune and Soneson, 1996). Lack of family support, lack of faculty and staff support, and the limited ability of overseas sites to accommodate students with disabilities have been identified as barriers to study abroad for students with disabilities (Hurst, 1998). The concerns identified in a survey of Big Ten study abroad and disability services staff were identifying accessible sites; determining the nature and scope of their institution's obligations to disabled students; providing specific types of accommodations, such as sign language interpreting and adaptive technology; and finding funds to assist students in meeting the extra costs associated with studying abroad with a disability (Aune and Soneson, 1996).

Strategies for Encouraging Participation. Successful strategies that include students with disabilities are implemented within existing study-abroad programs and ensure that reasonable accommodations are made within those programs. When surveyed, students with disabilities reported that they wanted to study abroad in mainstream programs, not programs specifically designed for students with disabilities (Matthews, Hameister, and Hosely, 1998).

To build student awareness of study-abroad opportunities, recruitment methods must be implemented that reflect the needs of students with disabilities, such as developing brochures and posters that illustrate people with disabilities studying and traveling abroad. A student advisory committee and peer mentors who are also students with disabilities and have traveled abroad are useful in helping prospective students explore options and determine what physical, programmatic, informational, and attitudinal barriers they may face when traveling abroad.

Because limited numbers of students with disabilities study abroad, disability service providers and study-abroad professionals have few opportunities to work together and learn about each other's fields. As a result, information that may prove useful and valuable to either professional group may not be known or shared, resulting in a lack of information provided to students that may inhibit opportunity.

To develop a coherent advising process, it is important for study-abroad advisers and disability specialists to work collaboratively and to understand each other's roles. Any student studying abroad must learn whether there are immunization requirements or specific government entry requirements (such as a visa or financial guarantee), an area of expertise for the study-abroad adviser (Hurst, 1998). This adviser can also provide essential information on the cultural context of the country the student intends to visit. The student, study-abroad adviser, and disability specialist must act as a team to identify and implement reasonable accommodations abroad and to differentiate between essential and preferred accommodations. Once the student's accommodation needs have been determined, study-abroad staff must notify the overseas site to confirm what accommodations can be provided. If accommodations cannot be provided, the team will need to identify alternative sites that do provide the accommodations necessary.

Providing Accommodations Abroad. It is important to understand the level of accessibility at key overseas sites. The University of Minnesota, Pennsylvania State University, and the Institute for the International Education of Students developed an Access Assessment as a mechanism for gathering this information. The Access Assessment is composed of checklists of the types of accommodations available for students with mobility, vision, hearing, learning, psychiatric, and cognitive disabilities in overseas classrooms, field trips, housing, food services, technology, campus support services, student life, library, transportation, and health services. To gain a culturally appropriate picture of the level of access, overseas sites are also asked how accommodations may typically be provided in their home countries. This information is made available to students, study-abroad advisers, and disability specialists through printed materials and the University of Minnesota's Global Campus and Disability Services' World Wide Web sites.

Cultural Context and Disability. Those who are advising students on study-abroad options must consider that a visible disability is not viewed similarly in all countries. For example, in some countries, disabilities may be viewed as a charity concern rather than a civil rights concern. In addition, how individuals with disabilities are accommodated varies by country. For example, in some South American countries, individual effort is used to propel a wheelchair or navigate inclines rather than power generated by motors or technology. It is therefore considered acceptable for someone using a wheelchair to be carried up a flight of stairs. Students with disabilities must consult with study-abroad advisers to understand the cultural context of the accommodation and whether they are comfortable with how accommodations are provided in a particular country.

Examples of Inclusiveness. The Ohio State University's Campus Collaboration Campaign is a cooperative program of the Office for Disability Services (ODS) and the Office for International Education's (OIE) Study Abroad Program. The program's goal is to increase the number of students with disabilities who participate in study-abroad experiences (M. Kinney, personal communication, Sept. 30, 1999).

This goal is accomplished in several ways. First, targeted recruitment efforts are completed by distributing program fliers at ODS and OIE, presenting at ODS New Student Orientations, and advertising the program on the ODS and OIE Web sites. Once students express interest in a particular study-abroad site, several meetings are conducted with the student and ODS and OIE staff to discuss site accessibility and to develop an accommodation plan for the site. After returning from abroad, the student meets with ODS and OIE staff to evaluate the experience. The student then has the option to serve as a mentor for other students with disabilities who wish to study abroad.

In addition to developing recruitment and advising plans, The Ohio State University Office for Student Affairs has set aside money to provide financial assistance to students with disabilities who wish to study abroad. The university plans to develop roundtable discussions with other international educators in Ohio to discuss ways to implement the program at other institutions (M. Kinney, personal communication, Sept. 30, 1999).

Augusta State University's Studies Abroad Office and Disability Services collaborated to develop Affirmative Study Abroad Programs (ASAP). Coordinators of both offices recognized the following barriers to study-abroad participation: the application process was not clear, the financial aid process was not initiated early enough, and students did not meet with the study-abroad contact for financial aid (D. Darris, personal communication, Sept. 30, 1999). The following solutions were implemented: study-abroad procedures were described on a flier distributed to students with disabilities, students were encouraged to apply for financial aid early, and students were referred directly to the study-abroad staff by the Disability Services coordinator.

Through ASAP, once the student decides to study abroad, he or she meets with a student who has studied abroad, develops a written success plan for studying abroad, and works with the Studies Abroad coordinator and Disability Services coordinator to explore community resources and how disability-related needs will be met in the host country (D. Darris, personal communication, Sept. 30, 1999). When the student returns to Augusta State University, he or she has the opportunity to serve as a peer support contact for other students with disabilities who wish to study abroad.

Sports and Recreation

The benefits of recreational activity include decreased levels of stress, an improved quality of life, better physical fitness, a sense of belonging, increased self-concept, a connection to one's community, and opportunities to meet others (Bryant, Banta, and Bradley, 1995; Seigenthaler, 1997). Many of these same benefits are gained by participation in team sports and are shared by individuals with or without disabilities (Schleien, Ray, and Green, 1997).

Despite the benefits associated with sports and recreation programs, few colleges, universities, and communities provide opportunities for students with disabilities to participate in such programs (Hedrick and Hedrick, 1993). Barriers to create these opportunities include physical, attitudinal, and administrative (Schleien, Germ, and McAvoy, 1996; Schleien, Ray, and Green, 1997).

Strategies for Encouraging Participation. To increase access to sports and recreation opportunities for students with disabilities, disability specialists should identify accessible programs and actively promote the use of facilities (Hedrick, 1994). They also must work with campus recreation programs to advocate the inclusion of accessible programs and services.

A campus recreation facility audit is an important starting point to determine accessibility of programs. Physical features that can be addressed in providing access include signage (such as raised lettering or braille signage), height of mounted lockers, width of shower or dressing stalls, access to shower stalls, access to pool entry, pool lifts, lips or steps to tennis or rac-quetball courts, height of gate latches and ease of manipulation for open-ing, and availability of adaptive equipment (Devine and Broach, 1998; Devine, McGovern, and Hermann, 1998).

Attitudinal barriers can be initially addressed through training of rec-reation and sport staff. Training must include sufficient information and skill (about disability awareness, accommodation strategies and techniques, and adaptive equipment) to work with and assist all members of the community in recreational pursuits (Devine and Broach, 1998; Devine, McGovern, and Hermann, 1998). Panel discussions by students with disabilities and their participation in sports and recreation can prove to be valuable training tools (Devine, McGovern, and Hermann, 1998). An explanation of person-first language (Dattilo and Smith, 1990) will assist staff in understanding its importance in creating an inclusive environment. Staff who assess their own attitudes about disability and model behavior in support of inclusion of stu-dents with disabilities will serve as powerful role models (Devine, McGovern, and Hermann, 1998).

It is essential to acknowledge inclusion as a priority in service delivery and reflect it in a mission statement, program goals, and objectives (Devine and Broach, 1998). Administrative policy review must be undertaken to determine if barriers to participation exist resulting from policy restrictions, patterns in the allocation of resources, or program limitations.

Disability support staff can assist in assessing inclusiveness by review-ing marketing tools used to solicit participation in recreational activities by all students. The distribution and location of marketing tools such as fliers and brochures and their availability in alternative format should be reviewed (Devine and Broach, 1998).

Examples of Inclusiveness. The Wisconsin Hoofers, a group com-posed of students with disabilities at the University of Wisconsin-Madison, is an outdoor recreation club with more than fifty-five hundred dues-paying student participants. The Hoofers encompasses the Riding, Mountaineer-ing, Sailing, Ski and Snowboard, Scuba, Gliding and Outing Clubs. Thus accessible outdoor recreational opportunities are varied and available to any student with a disability at the University of Wisconsin (T. Duffy, personal communication, Sept. 30, 1999). The Hoofers Club is organized, admin-istered, and maintained completely by students. Efforts to include students with disabilities were student initiated and implemented. The philosophy driving the Hoofers is, "Anyone can join, anyone can learn."

All specialty interest clubs within the general Hoofers Club have an accessibility component. The Ski and Snowboard Club, for example, col-laborates with the local school district's accessible recreation program and organizes monthly ski outings for any elementary, secondary, or postsec-ondary student with a disability who is interested in downhill skiing. Sit-down mono-skis assisted by able-bodied guides give many individuals their first downhill skiing experience. The Outdoor Club purchased tandem bikes for use by low-vision and blind students and a sighted riding partner. The Mountaineering Club has adaptive equipment and training opportunities for students with physical disabilities who want to scale high and rugged rock formations. In 1990, an Accessible Sailing Committee was organized by interested members of the Hoofer Sailing Club to expand sailing opportunities for individuals with disabilities.

The University of Arizona offers the Center for Disability-Related Resources, which provides a comprehensive program of competitive athletics and recreational activities to ensure equal access for students with disabilities to recreational sport activities (S. Kroeger, personal communication, Sept. 30, 1999). Arizona's wheelchair basketball team has competed since 1974 and plays approximately thirty games per season, primarily tournament play in the western region. Wildchair quad rugby started at the University of Arizona in 1989 but folded after two years of competition as a result of insufficient numbers of eligible players. It started up again in 1992 and plays at tournaments throughout the western region.

The university also sponsors a goal ball team for students who are blind and visually impaired. Sound is used so players can locate the ball, and scoring lines attached to the floor are raised to permit players to feel the boundaries and scoring area. This team plays in the southwestern region.

Conclusion

Students with disabilities face many challenges in completing their college degrees and obtaining meaningful employment. Providers of service play an integral role in helping students with disabilities obtain academic accommodations, which are vital in gaining access to the full range of academic experiences. They must also advocate that students with disabilities have access to out-of-class experiences, an important component for students' personal and professional development.

Campus life, experiential learning, study abroad, and sports and recreation programs build self-confidence and leadership, facilitate interpersonal relationships, and promote career development, which students will benefit from for the rest of their lives. It is the responsibility of disability service providers and student affairs professionals to ensure that students with disabilities have access to and become active participants in campus life.

References

Anderson, L., and others. "Creating Positive Change Through an Integrated Outdoor Adventure Program." *Therapeutic Recreation Journal*, 1997, *31*(4), 215–229.

Astin, A. W. *What Matters in College? Four Critical Years Revisited*. San Francisco: Jossey-Bass, 1993.

Aune, B. P., and Kroeger, S. A. "Career Development of College Students with Disabilities: An Interactional Approach to Defining the Issues." *Journal of College Student Development*, 1997, *38*(4), 345–355.

Aune, B. P., and Soneson, H. "Survey of CIC Institutions Concerning Study Abroad and Disability." Unpublished raw data, University of Minnesota, 1996.

Bryant, J. A., Banta, T. W., and Bradley, J. L. "Assessment Provides Insight into the Impact and Effectiveness of Campus Recreation Programs." *NASPA Journal*, 1995, 32(2) 153–160.

Bucks, C. *A World of Options: A Guide to International Exchange, Community Service and Travel for Persons with Disabilities.* Eugene, Oreg.: Mobility International USA, 1997.

Carnegie Foundation for the Advancement of Teaching. *Campus Life: In Search of Community.* Princeton, N.J.: Princeton University Press, 1990.

Chelberg, G., Harbour, W., and Juarez, R. L. *Accessing Student Life: Steps to Improve the Campus Climate for Disabled Students.* Minneapolis: University of Minnesota Disability Services, 1998. (ED 432 115)

Dattilo, J., and Murphy, W. D. "Facilitating the Challenge of Adventure Recreation for Persons with Disabilities." *Therapeutic Recreation Journal*, 1987, 21(3), 14–20.

Dattilo, J., and Smith, R. W. "Communicating Positive Attitudes Toward People with Disabilities Through Sensitive Terminology." *Therapeutic Recreation Journal*, 1990, 24(1), 8–17.

Devine, M. A., and Broach, E. "Inclusion in the Aquatic Environment." *Parks and Recreation*, 1998, 33(2), 64–72.

Devine, M. A., McGovern, J. N., and Hermann, P. "Inclusion." *Parks and Recreation*, 1998, 33(7), 68–76.

Frank, K., Karst, R., and Boles, C. "After Graduation: The Quest for Employment by Disabled College Graduates." *Journal of Applied Rehabilitation Counseling*, 1989, 4(4), 3–7.

Hedrick, B. *Sports and Exercise Programs for Persons with Physical Disabilities.* New York: Hatherleigh, 1994.

Hedrick, B., and Broadbent, E. "Predictors of Physical Activity Among University Graduates with Physical Disabilities." *Therapeutic Recreation Journal*, 1996, 30(2), 137–148.

Hedrick, B., and Hedrick, S. "The Undiscovered Athlete: A Perspective on Collegiate Sports for Persons with Disabilities." In J. Bryant and L. Kiefer (eds.), *Change and Human Dimension of Physical Activity: Proceedings.* Buffalo: State University of New York at Buffalo, 1993.

Henderson, C. *College Freshmen with Disabilities.* Washington, D.C.: American Council on Education, HEATH Resource Center, 1999.

Hitchings, W. E., and others. "Identifying the Career Development Needs of College Students with Disabilities." *Journal of College Student Development*, 1998, 39, 23–32.

Hurst, A. "Students with Disabilities and International Exchanges." In A. Hurst (ed.), *Higher Education and Disabilities: International Approaches.* Hants, England: Ashgate, 1998.

Jarrow, J. "Beyond Ramps: New Ways of Viewing Access." In S. Kroeger and J. Schuck (eds.), *Responding to Disability Issues in Student Affairs.* New Directions for Student Services, no. 64. San Francisco: Jossey-Bass, 1993.

Kauffmann, N. L., Martin, J. N., and Weaver, H. D. *Students Abroad: Strangers at Home.* Yarmouth, Me.: Intercultural Press, 1992.

Kuh, G. D. "The Other Curriculum: Out-of-Class Experiences Associated with Student Learning and Personal Development." *Journal of Higher Education*, 1995, 66, 123–155.

Kuh, G. D., Branch Douglas, K., Lund, J. P., and Raymin-Gyurnek, J. *Student Learning Outside the Classroom: Transcending Artificial Boundaries.* Washington, D.C.: George Washington University, 1994.

Kuh, G. D., and others. *Involving Colleges: Successful Approaches to Fostering Student Learning and Development Outside the Classroom.* San Francisco: Jossey-Bass, 1991.

Laycock, A. B., Hermon, M. V., and Laetz, V. "A Support Mechanism for the Worker with a Disability." *Journal of Rehabilitation*, 1992, 58, 56–62.

Lindquist, V. R. *Trends in the Employment of College and University Graduates in Business and Industry: The Northwestern Lindquist-Endicott Report 1992.* Evanston, Ill.: Placement Center of Northwestern University, 1993.

Matthews, P. R., Hameister, B. G., and Hosely, N. S. "Attitudes of College Students Toward Study Abroad: Implications for Disability Service Providers." *Journal of Postsecondary Education and Disability*, 1998, *13*(2) 67–73.

National Center for Education Statistics. *Students with Disabilities in Postsecondary Education*. Washington, D.C.: U.S. Department of Education, 1999.

Pace, C. R. *The Undergraduate: A Report of Their Activities and Progress in College in the 1980s*. Los Angeles: University of California at Los Angeles, Center for the Study of Evaluation, 1990.

Pascarella, E. T., and Terenzini, P. T. *How College Affects Students*. San Francisco: Jossey-Bass, 1991.

Schleien, S. J., Germ, P. A., and McAvoy, L. H. "Inclusive Community Leisure Services: Recommended Professional Practices and Barriers Encountered." *Therapeutic Recreation Journal*, 1996, *30*(2), 260–273.

Schleien, S. J., Ray, M. T., and Green, E. P. *Community Recreation and People with Disabilities: Strategies for Inclusion*. Baltimore, Md.: Paul H. Brookes, 1997.

Schuh, J. H., and Laverty, M. "The Perceived Long Term Effect of Holding a Significant Student Leadership Position." *Journal of College Student Personnel*, 1983, *24*, 28–32.

Seigenthaler, K. L. "Health Benefits of Leisure." *Parks and Recreation*, 1997, *32*(1), 24–31.

Stern, D., Hopkins, C., McMillion, M., and Cagampang, H. "Quality of Work Experience as Perceived by Two-Year College Students in Co-op and Non Co-op Jobs." *Journal of Cooperative Education*, 1992, *28*, 34–47.

Strange, C. C., and Banning, J. *Educating by Design: Creating Campus Environments That Work*. San Francisco: Jossey-Bass, 2000.

Thompson, A. R., and Dooley-Dickey, K. "Self-Perceived Job Search Skills of College Students with Disabilities." *Rehabilitation Counseling Bulletin*, 1994, *37*, 358–370.

Trach, J. S., and Harney, J. Y. "Impact of Co-operative Education on Career Development for Community College Students with and Without Disabilities." *Journal of Vocational Education Research*, 1998, *23*, 147–158.

Vickery, L. J., and McClure, M. D. *The 4 P's of Accessibility in Post-Secondary Education: Philosophy, Policy, Procedures, and Programs*. Muncie, Ind.: Ball State University, 1998. (ED 421 825)

DONNA JOHNSON *is assistant director of disability services at the University of Minnesota in Minneapolis.*

5

This chapter places the interactional model of disability in the context of student development theory, relates various service delivery approaches to the interactional model, and suggests how career and academic advisers can approach specific advising issues from an interactional perspective.

Career and Academic Advising

Betty Aune

Theories of integration (Tinto, 1993), involvement (Astin, 1993), and mattering (Schlossberg, Lynch, and Chickering, 1989) address the importance of the interaction between the student and the environment. From the perspective of the interactional model of disability, interactions between the individual and the campus environment have a profound influence on retention and completion for a disabled student. By placing disability in the context of student development theory, I seek to bring disability into the realm of the familiar for campus career and academic advisers. If advisers understand that they can apply theory they already know to students with disabilities, they may feel better equipped to handle issues brought by this group of students. This chapter relates the interactional model of disability to student development theory and various student services approaches, and suggests how career and academic advisers can approach specific advising issues from the interactional perspective.

Student Development Theory and the Interactional Model

The traditional approach to disability has been from a medical (functional limitations) frame: something is wrong with the student, and the expert's job is to return the individual to "normalcy." Normalcy, in the campus setting, has been accomplished by "remediating" the student to fit the campus environment. The interactional model stands in sharp contrast to the medical model. In the interactional (social constructivist) model, the interaction between an individual and the environment determines whether a characteristic becomes a disability. Jones (1996) stated, "To think of disability as a socially constructed phenomenon is to distinguish between the biological fact of disability and the handicapping social environment in which the person with disabilities exists" (p. 351). The environment bears as much responsibility for adjusting to disabled individuals as those individuals bear in adjusting to the environment (Gill, 1992).

The interactional model would suggest that academic and social integration, not normalization, is what students need to be successful in college. Such integration requires just as much adjustment by nondisabled students, faculty, and staff as by students with disabilities. Indeed, Enright, Conyers, and Szymanski (1996) identified the two factors "most critical to the integration of students with disabilities [as] (a) the ease of social interactions with peers and (b) the receptiveness of faculty members to accommodate their needs" (p. 106). This is not surprising, considering Tinto's (1993) research on the general student population, which found that students' experiences when interacting with the environment affect their goals of and commitments to college completion.

Campus involvement positively affects students' experience in college (Astin, 1993). Yet in a survey of 251 college and university students with disabilities on nine midwestern campuses, 84 percent indicated they were not at all involved in cocurricular activities (Johnson and others, 1998). Students with disabilities face frequent discrimination, negation of their goals, and organizational practices that limit accessibility, impeding their integration into the life of the institution. They often find themselves at the margin in systems that are inaccessible and unable or unwilling to adapt.

The Interactional Model and Approaches to Student Services

Current approaches to student services can be placed on a continuum in relation to the interactional model. At one extreme are decentralized services, in which academic advising, career advising, and disability services are provided separately, with no consultation among these offices. In a survey of 142 schools randomly selected from *Lovejoy's College Guide for the Learning Disabled,* 70 percent of the respondents reported that the career services and disability services offices operated completely autonomously (de Bettencourt, Bonaro, and Sabornie, 1995). This model is consistent with the medical model, in which the student is seen as deficient and in need of "fixing." In such a model, the burden is placed on the student to gain access to services, and the career services may not be appropriately adapted to the student with a disability (de Bettencourt, Bonaro, and Sabornie, 1995). Lack of communication between service providers was frustrating for students and resulted in ambiguity and ineffective services (Albert and Fairweather, 1990).

An alternative to this segmented approach is for the disability services office to provide all academic and career advising for students with disabilities. This model provides for easier access to services, but certainly does not further integrate the student into the life of the institution. And because the students are not given access to the same services as nondisabled students, it could be considered discriminatory under the guidelines of Section 504 and the Americans with Disabilities Act. It would be a rare disability services office that would have the resources or expertise to provide career counseling and placement services (Rabby and Croft, 1991).

A third alternative is for career and academic advising to work in collaboration with disability services. For example, disability services could provide training to staff or conduct an accessibility audit of their office. At the University of Arkansas, students with disabilities participate in integrated career exploration activities, but the Campus Access Office provides technical assistance on disability-related issues, such as disclosure, accommodations, privacy, and discrimination (Rumrill, Gordon, Brown, and Boen, 1994). This approach has the advantage of further integrating students with disabilities into the life of the campus community at the same time that they benefit from the expertise offered by both disability services and career advising.

Truly collaborative structures would lead to a fourth alternative, which is a service delivery system that is so well adapted that students with disabilities do not need any special services. This is the concept of universal design, in which services, facilities, programs, and attitudes take human variations into account. In universal design, environments and activities are designed in such a way that they are accessible to anyone, regardless of the person's functional limitations. Jones (1996) gave the example of service counters and bulletin boards that are low enough for wheelchair users. Another example is an auditorium in which any seat can be removed to accommodate a wheelchair and every seat has devices for hard-of-hearing individuals to enhance hearing and for blind individuals to hear descriptions of visual stimuli. The alternative is an auditorium in which the only place a wheelchair user can sit is in the front or in the back of the auditorium, a hard-of-hearing individual must have an interpreter, and a blind individual will not be aware of what is happening visually on stage. An example of universal design in programming is demonstrated in a study by Conyers and Szymanski (1998) in which students with and without disabilities participated in an integrated career planning intervention. The integrated intervention was effective for both groups of students. Truly integrated services, relevant for students with and without disabilities, are the most consistent with the spirit of the ADA, which mandates that services be provided in the most integrated setting possible.

Applying the Interactional Model to Specific Advising Issues

Universal design epitomizes the interactional model because the environment is adapted to individuals rather than requiring the individual to adapt to the environment. Academic and career advisers can effect a universal design in their services in a number of ways:

Recognize their assumptions about disability and how those assumptions affect their behavior toward students with disabilities (Fichten, 1988).

Create an atmosphere of mutual respect and trust (Rabby and Croft, 1991; Schriner and Roessler, 1990).

Understand how disability and the environment interact to create barriers (Aune and Kroeger, 1997; Enright, Conyers, and Szymanski, 1996; Murphy, 1992; Silver, Strehorn, and Bourke, 1997).

Use flexibility and creativity to solve problems (Enright, Conyers, and Szymanski, 1996; Murphy, 1992; Rabby and Croft, 1991).

Address disclosure issues (Enright, Conyers, and Szymanski, 1996; Friehe, Aune, and Leuenberger, 1996; Greenbaum, Graham, and Scales, 1996; Lynch and Gussel, 1996; Weiner and Wiener, 1996).

Achieve a balance in focus between disability issues and issues all students face (Fichten, Robillard, Tagalakis, and Amsel, 1991).

Balance support with fostering independence (Fichten and others, 1990; Strommer, 1995).

Recognize One's Assumptions and How Those Assumptions Affect One's Behavior. People with disabilities experience prejudice similar to that practiced against other groups. Professionals need to examine whether they actually hold unfavorable or even hostile attitudes toward a particular group (Schlossberg, Lynch, and Chickering, 1989). For example, they may assume that all disabled people are more dependent on others or that students with mental illness are more likely to be violent than others. It is not unusual for nondisabled people to assume that a person who is disabled in one area is also limited in other areas (Lynch and Gussel, 1996). For example, people who use wheelchairs are often spoken to as if they were children or hard of hearing. Students with disabilities frequently receive accolades for accomplishing something for which nondisabled students would not even be recognized. Such behavior implies that students with disabilities are not expected to achieve at the same level as nondisabled students. Subtle behaviors such as these, which the nondisabled person may not even recognize as a form of stereotyping, are as prejudiced as overtly hostile behavior. Most troubling to many students with invisible disabilities is the fact that some faculty and staff simply do not believe the student has a disability (Litsheim, 1995). Indeed, Greenbaum, Graham, and Scales (1995) reported, "The most common institutional barrier to success cited by students with disabilities was lack of understanding and cooperation from faculty and administrators, including discrimination because of the participants' disability" (p. 468).

It is important to emphasize that one's practices must be examined as rigorously as one's attitudes. Just because someone espouses positive attitudes toward disabled people does not mean that those attitudes are reflected in his or her practice (Cook, 1992). For example, MacLean and Gannon (1997) found that positive attitudes toward disability did not translate to actual support for university students with emotional disabilities. Other studies too have reported that faculty were less likely to initiate discussion with a student with a disability about an academic problem than with a non-disabled student (Fichten and others, 1990), and people who do initiate contact with a disabled person sometimes experience strain, therefore ending their interaction with the person more quickly than with a nondisabled person (Cook, 1992).

Suggestions for counteracting one's own prejudices and assumptions include understanding the dynamics at work in one's interactions with disabled people (Cook, 1992); seeking equal status contact with people with disabilities by hiring people with disabilities (offering the opportunity for student services staff to work alongside disabled colleagues); inviting people with disabilities to sit on advisory boards; and inviting employers with disabilities to speak to student groups (Aune and Kroeger, 1997). Such actions, if done only on a token basis, may have little or even a negative effect. However, if such actions become part of a pattern of inclusiveness of people with disabilities, they may eventually lead to more positive attitudes and better understanding. Contact reduces stereotyping only if it is the right kind of contact (Coryell, Holcomb, and Scherer, 1992). The contact should be frequent and close, with pursuit of shared goals, and with equal status for group members.

Create an Atmosphere of Mutual Respect and Trust. Career and academic advisers who wish to work toward establishing mutual respect and trust will need to listen to the students' own descriptions of the barriers they have encountered and possible solutions. Affirming students' self-assessment is an important step in achieving mutual respect (Aune and Kroeger, 1997; Rabby and Croft, 1991; Schriner and Roessler, 1990). For example, in their interviews with thirteen university students, Aune and Kroeger (1997) concluded that what this group of students found most helpful "was to receive individualized, personal support, and to be respected, valued and accepted" (p. 353). Weiner and Wiener (1996) found that students with psychiatric disabilities were much more likely to use the academic advising services if they could meet with the same adviser over an extended period of time.

Behaviors ranked important by 80 percent or more in a study of 1,448 college students with disabilities on eighty-seven campuses in thirty-nine states were being treated with respect by service providers, being encouraged to develop all their skills and to develop career plans, having their needs considered in the design of career training programs, being expected by faculty to succeed in college, being encouraged to train for the professions and prepare for a wide range of jobs, and being encouraged to participate in interviews with employers (Schriner and Roessler, 1990). All of these behaviors imply respect for individuals and belief in their potential. Rabby and Croft (1991) described this atmosphere as carrying with it "an aura of welcome" in which the student with a disability "is treated as a natural part of the career planning and placement program" (p. 51).

Creating such an environment of respect and trust is not easy. Nutter and Ringgenberg (1993) suggested that things as simple as displaying artwork that includes disabled people and having devices such as a TDD (telecommunications device for the deaf) send a message that students with disabilities are valued. A university student who was interviewed about the support she had received described how she had experienced such an environment, "Your opinion is valued. It's not like they come in and tell you what to do. They ask you what you think, and you're part of the team. There was acceptance of capability within disability" (Aune and Kroeger, 1997, p. 349).

Understand Disability-Related and Environmental Barriers. The time of onset of disability affects the kinds of barriers a student with a disability experiences (Hershenson and Szymanski, 1992). Students with congenital disabilities may have had fewer work experiences than nondisabled students or may have been excluded from critical developmental activities, such as job shadowing experiences in middle school or hearing their parents and teachers express hopes and aspirations for them. But many individuals with acquired disabilities need to establish new identities as disabled persons and adjust their conception of their life goals. They may lose trust in their skills and problem-solving ability (Aune and Kroeger, 1997; Enright, Conyers, and Szymanski, 1996). Many students with disabilities experience career indecision (Conyers and Szymanski, 1998).

Considering the identity development and goal-setting needs for students with congenital and acquired disabilities, student services professionals may wonder why many students with disabilities do not take advantage of services their office provides. Recent studies have found that between 15 and 37 percent of college graduates with disabilities at three large universities used the career counseling services at their university; 57 to 66 percent of the general student population at the same institutions had used the services (Friehe, Aune, and Leuenberger, 1996; Silver, Strehorn, and Bourke, 1997). Students in the study by Friehe, Aune, and Leuenberger indicated that they did not think they needed the services (61 percent), did not know of the services (23 percent), or did not think the services would be helpful (15 percent). Aune and Kroeger (1997) also found that some students who had had unpleasant experiences in one campus office assumed they would have similar experiences in other offices and therefore did not even try the career services on campus.

Most important, students with disabilities face attitudinal barriers and occasionally outright discrimination in both academic and employment settings. For example, in a survey of 761 college and university students with disabilities from forty-three institutions in Virginia, a large number of the students cited social isolation, ostracism, and scorn from instructors and fellow students due to their disability (West and others, 1993). Several other studies reported that negative attitudes held by faculty and staff as well as students served as major barriers to the academic and social integration of students with disabilities (Fichten, Robillard, Judd, and Amsel, 1989; Foster and Brown, 1989; Litsheim, 1995). In a study of a college community that included both deaf and hearing individuals, poor modeling by hearing faculty, staff, and administrators was cited by hearing students as a factor in the development of negative attitudes toward deaf students (Coryell, Holcomb, and Scherer, 1992). In a survey of Canadian university students from twenty-one institutions in eight provinces, one-third of respondents reported that not receiving accommodations from instructors had seriously impeded their ability to succeed at the university (Hill, 1996). Perhaps most alarming was a study of college and university students with disabilities at nine midwestern institutions conducted over three years, in which 25 to 33 percent of the students reported having been discriminated against or harassed on campus because of their disability. Over the three years, 52 to 62 percent reported professors as a source of discrimination, 24 to 31 percent reported staff, and 47 to 54 percent reported other students (Johnson and others, 1998).

Career and academic advisers need to consider carefully whether they are more likely to discourage students with a disability from pursuing their career goals than nondisabled students. Studies involving fourteen Canadian and two large American institutions reported that faculty believed that a disability could limit appropriate majors for a student and had discouraged students with disabilities from pursuing their chosen field (Hill, 1994; Houck, Asselin, Troutman, and Arrington, 1992; Silver, Strehorn, and Bourke, 1997). In the study by Silver, Strehorn, and Bourke, 32 percent of college graduates with a variety of disabilities reported they were discouraged from pursuing their preferred major. These authors suggested that ways "that are not discouraging" (p. 525) be found to provide realistic advice to students with disabilities. For example, advisers can encourage students to balance their course load, so that they do not take more than one course per term in their weakest area. They can suggest that students consider how many times per week the class meets and how long the sessions are. Students may be more successful in a particular course with more frequent and shorter class sessions. Students have suggested that faculty not discourage them from taking courses that may pose barriers, but instead tell students about potential problems in taking the particular course and then let students make their own decisions (Fichten and others, 1990).

Use Flexibility and Creativity. Instead of discouraging students, the adviser should work collaboratively with the student and other professionals involved to solve problems, find accommodations, and create a more universally designed environment. Rabby and Croft (1991) supported the notion of flexibility, "A good career services office is flexible and responsive. It should make few, if any, across-the-board decisions when planning services for disabled students. The office is most effective when it treats each student, disabled or non-disabled, as a one-of-a-kind case study" (p. 50).

Treating each student as an individual requires asking students about the kinds of accommodations they desire rather than making assumptions about what they need (Fichten and others, 1990; Enright, Conyers, and Szymanski, 1996). In some cases, the student may opt not to take advantage of accommodations that to the adviser seem clearly needed. However, the student is not obligated to use every accommodation offered. At the same time, the student does not necessarily have a right to every accommodation he or she requests. Consultation with the disability services office is essential whenever an adviser questions the appropriateness of a particular accommodation for a student.

Many, if not most, solutions to access problems can be solved by either simple adjustments to the environment or compensatory strategies that the disabled person uses. Students and workers compensate for the inaccessibility of their environment many times a day. For example, taking extra time and monitoring their work are typical strategies that adults with learning disabilities use in work settings (Adelman and Vogel, 1990; Murphy, 1992). The three most common strategies that adults with learning disabilities use (getting help from their peers, organizing the environment, and concealing the disability) are basically ignored by professional advisers as legitimate strategies (Murphy, 1992). Advisers need to recognize that such compensatory strategies may be the most effective in environments in which the disability carries a social stigma.

One of the most difficult accommodations to consider is modified assessment. Modified assessment includes any adaptation that alters testing format or procedures but not content; for example, extended time for completing the test, having the test read out loud, having a scribe, giving oral instead of written answers, and taking the test in a separate room. Career advisers need to consider such modifications when they conduct career assessment with students with disabilities or advise students regarding licensure or employment testing. The American Psychological Association's Division for Evaluation, Measurement and Statistics (Enright, Conyers, and Szymanski, 1996) came to the conclusion that tests given under modified conditions cannot be mathematically compared to tests given under standardized conditions, and they probably do not measure the constructs for which the test was developed. In contrast, not using modifications such as extended time may make the measure less valid for individuals with learning or psychiatric disabilities who experience heightened anxiety during testing (Hoy and others, 1997). In addition, tests that were not normed on a population with specific disabilities may not be valid for individuals with those disabilities. Parker and Schaller (1996) therefore recommended that advisers consider alternative assessment procedures with disabled individuals, such as self-reports, criterion assessments, ecological assessments, and qualitative assessments.

Career counselors should consult with students regarding test accommodation options, determine what past accommodations have been used, read guidelines for fair testing, choose criterion-referenced over norm-referenced tests, consider students' life experiences when interpreting results, and consider how his or her own perception of the student's disability is affecting the interpretation (Enright, Conyers, and Szymanski, 1996). The adviser should also consult with the disability services office about appropriate test accommodations for a particular student, and the disability services office should handle any test accommodation requests for academic course work.

In some cases, test results are flagged when they are achieved under nonstandard conditions. The American Psychological Association concluded that flagging these scores raises complex ethical issues. A student who wishes to have accommodations needs to determine whether those accommodations will be made known to the potential user of the test results (in some cases, the user may be a licensing board or potential employer). The student can then make an informed decision as to whether to use the accommodation (Phillips, 1994).

Address Disclosure Issues. Students with hidden disabilities represent by far the largest group of students with disabilities. Yet these students frequently do not disclose their disability for fear of subsequent negative attitudes and behaviors toward them. Students with psychiatric disabilities are especially reluctant to disclose because of the stigma associated with mental illness and their desire to prove they can be successful on their own (Weiner and Wiener, 1996). Similar reluctance has been reported in terms of disclosure to employers (Friehe, Aune, and Leuenberger, 1996; Greenbaum, Graham, and Scales, 1996; Silver, Strehorn, and Bourke, 1997). A major reason for not disclosing was fear of discrimination.

Advisers cannot be expected to accommodate disabilities of which they are not even aware. However, mutual respect and trust should provide the environment in which a student would be willing to disclose to the adviser. Once a student has disclosed, the adviser can help the student consider the advantages and disadvantages of disclosing in different situations, such as classrooms, internships, and employment settings. Factors that students need to consider are what information is essential in order to receive desired accommodations and how much they are comfortable revealing, which may vary depending on their relationship with the person to whom they disclose and past experiences they may have had in disclosing to others.

Achieve Balance in Focus. Research indicates that a nondisabled person's natural inclination is to focus on the disability rather than on the person (Fichten, Robillard, Tagalakis, and Amsel, 1991). Although their thoughts may be focused on the disability, advisers are frequently hesitant to discuss the disability openly. They need to find a balance between ignoring the disability and focusing entirely on it. The impact of the disability and of the institution's (or potential employer's) response to the disability must be addressed, but so too should all of the other issues a college student brings to the advising session—for example, trying to decide on a major, reconsidering a career goal, and choosing a good balance of courses for the upcoming semester.

In some cases, an adviser is aware of a disability, but the student does not bring it up when facing academic problems. In this case, it is advisable to talk with the student about how he or she perceives the effect the disability or the environment's impact on the disability has on the academic problems. If the student recounts problems getting accommodations in academic settings, the adviser and student should consult with the disability services office.

Balance Support with Fostering Independence. Strommer (1995, pp. 25–26) listed five levels of advising:

1. Providing basic information about courses and curricula.
2. Individualizing the academic program.
3. Assisting the student in identifying educational goals and in achieving them through institutional resources.
4. Fostering students' capacity for lifelong learning by developing advising tasks that teach goal setting, planning, and decision making and that provide practice in gathering and synthesizing information.
5. Creating a loop through which information about a changing student body and students' backgrounds, expectations, and goals may influence classroom practices, student learning, and campus life.

According to Strommer, many advisers do not go past the first two levels of advising, when, in fact, students from special populations (including those with disabilities) most need the kind of advising in levels three through five. She suggested that special populations of students need regular structured contact with their adviser. Aune and Kroeger (1997) found that students wanted "strong guidance, but also respect for their own autonomy" (p. 353).

Although some students with disabilities need structured and intense advising, they also need experience in managing their own affairs and making their own decisions. Finding the right balance between offering support and fostering independence is critically important in working with students with disabilities. Indeed, Gerber, Ginsberg, and Reiff (1992) found that highly successful adults with learning disabilities were those who had accepted their disabilities, were aware of their strengths and limitations, and were skilled at problem solving. Yet many students do not understand the impact their disability may have in relation to career development (Hitchings and others, 1998). They have frequently grown up with more support than the typical student. Their parents may have been more involved as participants in meetings at school and in advocating for services for their child. In addition, the K–12 system is under a legal obligation to find students with disabilities, determine what services they need, and provide them. These students are not necessarily prepared for the postsecondary system, in which it is their responsibility to self-identify and request the accommodations they need.

Another issue that advisers occasionally encounter is that of boundaries. How much caring is too much? How much adapting is too much? These are questions that advisers should be continually asking lest they go overboard to help and in the process encourage "learned helplessness," which can be seen as patronizing and demeaning to students (Fichten and others, 1990). The adviser should frequently ask himself or herself, "Is this something the student could be doing for himself or herself?" "Am I overprotecting the student?" "Is the adapting I am doing an imposition on someone else's standards or expectations for behavior?" If the answer to any of these questions is yes, the adviser may have overstepped the boundary between support and independence. But a student who has identified himself or herself and requested certain accommodations should not be expected to do this time and again with each instructor each term. The disability services office should play a role in facilitating accommodations that will be required repeatedly.

All of these suggestions can be considered, but the right step to take will depend on individual students and the context in which they find themselves. Career and academic advisers should consult with disability services staff when in doubt about appropriate accommodations and special considerations.

Conclusion

The interactional model of disability is compatible with current student development theory, which places an emphasis on the academic and social integration of students into campus life. Students with disabilities face numerous barriers in achieving such integration. Academic and career advisers have a unique opportunity to bring their institutions closer to universal design by examining their own attitudes and practices, establishing mutual respect and trust with students with disabilities, understanding how disability and institution interact to create barriers, using flexibility and creativity to solve problems, addressing disclosure issues, achieving a balance in focus between disability-related and nondisability-related issues, and balancing support with fostering independence for students with disabilities.

References

Adelman, P., and Vogel, S. "College Graduates with Learning Disabilities—Employment Attainment and Career Patterns." *Learning Disability Quarterly,* 1990, *13,* 154–166.

Albert, J. J., and Fairweather, J. S. "Effective Organization of Postsecondary Services for Students with Disabilities." *Journal of College Student Development,* 1990, *31,* 445–453.

Astin, A. W. *What Matters in College? Four Critical Years Revisited.* San Francisco: Jossey-Bass, 1993.

Aune, B., and Kroeger, S. "Career Development of College Students with Disabilities: An Interactional Approach to Defining the Issues." *Journal of College Student Development,* 1997, *38*(4), 344–355.

Conyers, L. M., and Szymanski, E. M. "The Effectiveness of Integrated Career Intervention for College Students with and Without Disabilities." *Journal of Postsecondary Education and Disability,* 1998, *13*(1), 23–34.

Cook, D. "Psychosocial Impact of Disability." In R. M. Parker and E. M. Szymanski (eds.), *Rehabilitation Counseling: Basics and Beyond.* (2nd ed.) Austin, Tex.: Pro-Ed, 1992.

Coryell, J., Holcomb, T. K., and Scherer, M. "Attitudes Toward Deafness: A Collegiate Perspective." *American Annals of the Deaf,* 1992, *137*, 299–302.

de Bettencourt, L. U., Bonaro, D. A., and Sabornie, E. J. "Career Development Services Offered to Postsecondary Students with Learning Disabilities." *Learning Disabilities Research and Practice,* 1995, *10*(2), 102–107.

Enright, M. S., Conyers, L. M., and Szymanski, E. M. "Career and Career-Related Educational Concerns of College Students with Disabilities." *Journal of Counseling and Development,* 1996, *75*, 103–114.

Fichten, C. S. "Students with Physical Disabilities in Higher Education: Attitudes and Beliefs That Affect Integration." In H. E. Yuker (ed.), *Attitudes Toward Disabled Persons.* New York: Springer, 1988.

Fichten, C. S., Robillard, K., Judd, D., and Amsel, R. "College Students with Physical Disabilities: Myths and Realities." *Rehabilitation Psychology,* 1989, *34*(4), 243–257.

Fichten, C. S., Robillard, K., Tagalakis, V., and Amsel, R. "Casual Interaction Between College Students with Various Disabilities and Their Nondisabled Peers: The Internal Dialogue." *Rehabilitation Psychology,* 1991, *36*(1), 3–20.

Fichten, C. S., and others. "Getting Along in College: Recommendations for College Students with Disabilities and Their Professors." *Rehabilitation Counseling Bulletin,* 1990, *34*(2), 103–125.

Foster, S., and Brown, P. "Factors Influencing the Academic and Social Integration of Hearing Impaired College Students," *Journal of Postsecondary Education and Disability,* 1989, *7*, 78–96.

Friehe, M., Aune, B., and Leuenberger, J. "Career Service Needs of College Students with Disabilities." *Career Development Quarterly,* 1996, *44*, 289–300.

Gerber, P., Ginsberg, R., and Reiff, H. "Identifying Alterable Patterns in Employment Success for Highly Successful Adults with Learning Disabilities." *Journal of Learning Disabilities,* 1992, *25*, 475–487.

Gill, C. J. "Valuing Life with a Disability: New Models for Modern Medicine." Paper presented at Americans with Disabilities: Introduction to an Emerging People, University of Minnesota, Minneapolis, 1992.

Greenbaum, B., Graham, S., and Scales, W. "Adults with Learning Disabilities: Educational and Social Experiences During College." *Exceptional Children,* 1995, *61*(5), 460–471.

Greenbaum, B., Graham, S., and Scales, W. "Adults with Learning Disabilities: Occupational and Social Status After College." *Journal of Learning Disabilities,* 1996, *29*(2), 167–173.

Hershenson, D. B., and Szymanski, E. M. "Career Development of People with Disabilities." In R. M. Parker and E. M. Szymanski (eds.), *Rehabilitation Counseling: Basics and Beyond.* (2nd ed.) Austin, Tex.: Pro-Ed, 1992.

Hill, J. L. "Speaking Out: Perceptions of Students with Disabilities at Canadian Universities Regarding Institutional Policies." *Journal of Postsecondary Education and Disability,* 1994, *11*(1), 1–14.

Hill, J. L. "Speaking Out: Perceptions of Students with Disabilities Regarding Adequacy of Services and Willingness of Faculty to Make Accommodations." *Journal of Postsecondary Education and Disability,* 1996, *12*(1), 22–43.

Hitchings, W. E., and others. "Identifying the Career Development Needs of College Students with Disabilities." *Journal of College Student Development,* 1998, *39*(1), 23–32.

Houck, C. K., Asselin, S. B., Troutman, G. C., and Arrington, J. M. "Students with Learn-ing Disabilities in the University Environment: A Study of Faculty and Student Per-ceptions." *Journal of Learning Disabilities,* 1992, *25*(10), 678–684.

Hoy, C., and others. "Depression and Anxiety in Two Groups of Adults with Learning Disabilities." *Learning Disability Quarterly,* 1997, *20,* 280–291.

Johnson, D., and others. *Engage: Disability Access to Student Life: Final Report.* Min-neapolis: Disability Services, University of Minnesota, 1998.

Jones, S. R. "Toward Inclusive Theory: Disability as Social Construction." *NASPA Jour-nal,* 1996, *33*(4), 347–354.

Litsheim, M. E. "Reflecting Disability Perspectives in the University of Minnesota (Twin Cities)." *Delta Pi Epsilon Journal,* 1995, *37*(3), 115–127.

Lynch, R. T., and Gussel, L. "Disclosure and Self-Advocacy Regarding Disability-Related Needs: Strategies to Maximize Integration in Postsecondary Education." *Journal of Counseling and Development,* 1996, *74,* 352–357.

MacLean, D., and Gannon, P. M. "The Emotionally Affected University Student: Sup-port from the University Community." *International Journal of Disability, Development and Education,* 1997, *44*(3), 217–228.

Murphy, S. T. *On Being L.D., Perspectives and Strategies of Young Adults.* New York: Teachers College Press, 1992.

Nutter, K. J., and Ringgenberg, L. J. "Creating Positive Outcomes for Students with Dis-abilities." In S. Kroeger and J. Schuck (eds.), *Responding to Disability Issues in Student Affairs.* New Directions for Student Services, no. 64. San Francisco: Jossey-Bass, 1993.

Parker, R. M., and Schaller, J. L. "Issues in Vocational Assessment and Disability." In E. M. Szymanski and R. M. Parker (eds.), *Work and Disability: Issues and Strategies in Career Development and Job Placement.* Austin, Tex.: Pro-Ed, 1996.

Phillips, S. E. "High-Stakes Testing Accommodations: Validity Versus Disabled Rights." *Applied Measurement in Education,* 1994, *7*(2), 93–120.

Rabby, R., and Croft, D. "Working with Disabled Students: Some Guidelines." *Journal of Career Planning and Employment,* 1991, *5*(2), 49–54.

Rumrill, P. D., Gordon, S. E., Brown, P. L., and Boen, L. L. "Transition to-and-from Higher Education: Toward a Model of Career Development Services for Students with Disabilities." *Journal of Cooperative Education,* 1994, *30*(1), 36–45.

Schlossberg, N. K., Lynch, A. Q., and Chickering, A. W. *Improving Higher Education Environments for Adults.* San Francisco: Jossey-Bass, 1989.

Schriner, K. F., and Roessler, R. T. "Employment Concerns of College Students with Dis-abilities: Toward an Agenda for Policy and Practice." *Journal of College Student Devel-opment,* 1990, *31*(4), 307–312.

Silver, P., Strehorn, K. C., and Bourke, A. "The 1993 Employment Follow-Up Study of Selected Graduates with Disabilities." *Journal of College Student Development,* 1997, *38*(5), 520–526.

Strommer, D. W. "Advising Special Populations of Students." In A. G. Reinarz and E. R. White (eds.), *Teaching Through Academic Advising: A Faculty Perspective.* New Direc-tions for Teaching and Learning, no. 62. San Francisco: Jossey-Bass, 1995.

Tinto, V. *Leaving College: Rethinking the Causes and Cures of Student Attrition.* (2nd ed.) Chicago: University of Chicago Press, 1993.

Weiner, E., and Wiener, J. "Concerns and Needs of University Students with Psychiat-ric Disabilities." *Journal of Postsecondary Education and Disability,* 1996, *12*(1), 2–9.

West, M., and others. "Beyond Section 504: Satisfaction and Empowerment of Students with Disabilities in Higher Education." *Exceptional Children,* 1993, *59*(5), 456–467.

BETTY AUNE is chair of the Education Department and assistant professor at the College of St. Scholastica in Duluth, Minnesota. She was previously associate director of disability services at the University of Minnesota-Twin Cities.

6

Since the passage of the Americans with Disabilities Act, issues unforeseen by the sponsors and proponents of this legislation have arisen. Issues such as definition and documentation of disability and access to standardized testing are being played out across the country, with mixed results.

Legal Issues in Serving Students with Disabilities in Postsecondary Education

Jo Anne Simon

Since the passage of Section 504 of the Rehabilitation Act of 1973 and the Americans with Disabilities Act (ADA), institutions have been engaged in an ongoing effort to establish precisely how to balance the rights of students with disabilities with those of the resources and obligations of postsecondary institutions. This chapter highlights key points in this dialogue. It also touches on unanticipated issues that have become central to the discussion since the ADA's passage by discussing court cases and letters of finding issued by the U.S. Department of Education, Office of Civil Rights (OCR). The ADA and Section 504 are substantially the same as they apply to higher education (*Guckenberger v. Trustees of Boston University*, 1997). Therefore this chapter will refer to either the ADA or Section 504.

General Obligations

Under Section 504, an institution's fundamental obligation is to avoid, or cease acting, in a discriminatory manner. But what exactly constitutes discrimination? Beyond obvious actions reflecting animus (ill will) or those decisions based on negative stereotypes regarding the skills and abilities of individuals with disabilities, it may be difficult for faculty and staff to identify, and thus avoid, discriminatory actions or decisions. Section 504 and the ADA prohibit actions that do the following:

Deny qualified students with disabilities the opportunity to participate in
programs or activities.

Provide aids and services that are not "equal to" or as "effective as" those
provided to others.

Provide different or separate aids, services, or benefits than those necessary
for providing meaningful access.

Provide significant assistance to third parties that discriminate against qualified individuals with disabilities.

Use methods of administration that result in discrimination.

Use eligibility criteria that screen out or tend to screen out individuals with
disabilities.

Fail to provide reasonable accommodations (*Soileau v. Maine,* 1997).

The laws also make clear that regardless of intent or animus, actions or
inactions that have the effect of discriminating against persons with disabilities are forbidden (*Pushkin v. University of Colorado,* 1981).

These obligations extend to all services, benefits, programs, opportunities, and activities of the institution in order to address discrimination
"stemming . . . from simple prejudice," as well as that which is the consequence of refusing to provide reasonable accommodations. Policies, practices, or procedures that exclude students with disabilities, or that deny
opportunities or benefits to qualified students with disabilities on the basis
of fear, speculation, or stereotypical attitudes, or that result in students with
disabilities being treated differently from similarly situated nondisabled students are prohibited.

The law imposes not only a prohibition against discrimination but also,
in appropriate circumstances, a positive obligation to make "reasonable
accommodation." Section 504 provides that "recipients . . . shall make such
modifications to its academic requirements as are necessary to ensure that
such requirements do not discriminate or have the effect of discriminating,
on the basis of disability" (34 C.F.R. sec. 104.44(a)). The Supreme Court in
Alexander v. Choate (1985) elaborated, "The benefit itself, of course, cannot
be defined in a way that effectively denies otherwise qualified handicapped
individuals the meaningful access to which they are entitled, to assure
meaningful access, reasonable accommodations in the grantee's program or
benefit may have to be made" (p. 301). Thus "meaningful access" requires
institutions to modify their programs and services to provide accommodations to students with disabilities.

Other general obligations include a requirement that postsecondary
institutions have an internal grievance policy and procedure that is consistent with notions of due process and is applicable to students with disabilities. The OCR has found that grievance policies must also cover admissions
and readmissions processes and must be published in a manner that ensures
adequate notice (*University of Oregon,* 1996).

Case law emanating from OCR clarifies that standard policies and procedures for responding to requests for accommodations must also be adopted. Institutions must develop a process for determining whether or what accommodations are to be provided, as well as a formal mechanism for ensuring that the accommodations are actually provided (*Cleveland Chiropractic College*, 1995).

Who Is Protected

Section 504 and the ADA define an individual with a disability as one who (a) has a physical or mental impairment that substantially limits a major life activity, (b) has a record of having such an impairment, or (c) is regarded as having such an impairment. Major life activities are "those basic activities that the average person . . . can perform with little or no difficulty" (29 C.F.R. Part 1630). The regulations contain an illustrative list—hearing, seeing, speaking, walking, breathing, learning, working, caring for oneself, and performing manual tasks (28 C.F.R. sec. 35.104). Courts have expanded the list to include sitting and standing, thinking, reading, sleeping, engaging in sexual relations and interacting with others, reproduction and writing, studying, and test taking. In order to be protected by the laws, students with disabilities must be "qualified," that is, able to meet the technical and academic qualifications for entry into the school or program (34 C.F.R. sec. 104.3 (k)(3)).

"Substantially limits" is defined as "significantly restrict[ed] as to the condition, manner or duration under which an individual can perform a particular major life activity as compared to the condition, manner, or duration under which most people can perform those activities (28 C.F.R. sec. 35.104 App. A, sec. 36.104 App. B). The issue of what is substantial has come under intense scrutiny. According to a minority of courts, postsecondary students with disabilities, who must be able to meet the academic and technical standards of the academic program, would, at the same time, be required to perform at a level below that of the average person, a seeming contradiction. The case most often cited for this proposition is *Price v. National Board of Medical Examiners* (1997), in which the district court held that three medical students with Attention Deficit Hyperactivity Disorder (ADHD) were not disabled under the ADA because their history of academic success belied a finding of disability. Two recent cases, *Gonzalez v. National Board of Medical Examiners* (1999) and *Doe v. National Board of Medical Examiners* (1999), produced contradictory results. Gonzalez was denied a preliminary injunction, and Doe was granted one. Both cases are pending appeal.

Other courts and OCR have found that the correct comparison is not to most people's achieved performance, but to the condition, manner, or duration in which most people perform the major life activities in question.

This view is consistent with the ADA's legislative history and the regulations and guidance promulgated by the U.S. Department of Justice. A case supporting this interpretation is *Bartlett v. New York State Board of Law Examiners* (1998). *Bartlett* is on remand to the Second Circuit Court of Appeals and appears to be consistent with recent Supreme Court rulings in *Sutton v. United Airlines, Inc.* (1999), *Murphy v. United Parcel Service, Inc.* (1999), and *Albertsons, Inc. v. Kirkingburg* (1999), in which the U.S. Supreme Court ruled that, contrary to the legislative history and a significant majority of federal courts of appeals, whether a person has a disability under the law must be assessed by considering the effects of mitigating measures, such as prosthetic devices or medications.

The postsecondary population most likely affected by these decisions are students with ADHD and psychological disabilities who might, with medication, be able to function like most other people. However, the Supreme Court cautioned that the mere use of mitigating measures does not mean that the person would not be disabled for purposes of the statute. Indeed, the Court pointed out that adverse effects of using mitigation measures, such as medication, must be considered as well.

Family Educational Rights and Privacy Act

Commonly known as the Buckley Amendment, the Family Educational Rights and Privacy Act (FERPA) is the primary federal statute affecting disclosure of educational records, including records that may reflect disability and related information in higher education. This statute protects students in two ways: students have access to their educational records, and unauthorized disclosures to persons without a legitimate educational interest are prohibited. Access to psychological treatment records is specifically exempted from such disclosure. Conversations with students with disabilities and observations by faculty and staff are not within the reach of FERPA, but may be governed by the ADA, Section 504, or state confidentiality laws, as well as state laws regarding privileged communications, such as those between doctors and patients.

Individuals with Disabilities Education Act

The Individuals with Disabilities Education Act (IDEA) is a federal special education statute that does not cover postsecondary educational institutions, but because it is the primary statute governing the educational programming of elementary and high school students with disabilities, parents, school officials, guidance counselors, and students have many misconceptions of students rights and responsibilities in higher education.

The IDEA establishes specific procedural safeguards and the right to free, appropriate public education in the least restrictive environment. Section 504 and the ADA provide that qualified persons with disabilities cannot be excluded from participation in, denied the benefits of, or be subjected to discrimination by any service, program, or activity of a postsecondary institution, and further provide that services must be provided in the "most integrated setting" (*Olmstead v. Zimring*, 1999). The IDEA requires only that special educational services ensure a meaningful benefit from education. Section 504 and the ADA are designed to provide only equivalent access to educational and extracurricular programs and opportunities, not specialized education, such as individualized tutoring.

One of the primary differences between the two statutes is the level of student responsibility. Under the IDEA, the disabled student is legally required to do no more than that required of other youngsters: go to school. Under Section 504 and the ADA, however, students themselves are responsible for quite a bit more. Students must disclose disability to an appropriate college official, usually the disability services office; provide appropriate documentation of disability; and act to facilitate the provision of reasonable accommodations. Students are responsible for speaking up if a problem arises. There is no statutory mechanism requiring parental involvement, and such involvement is generally discouraged in college.

Access to Postsecondary Education

Access has many faces, from the removal of physical barriers to providing communications access in programs and activities.

Physical Access: Off-Campus Buildings and Facilities. Students with disabilities must be given access to off-campus buildings and facilities that are being used in connection with the college's courses or extracurricular activities. So, for example, if Aqua-fer College does not have a swimming pool but contracts with the local YWCA for use by students at the college, Aqua-fer must provide equal access to the Y's pool, whether through retrofitting or adding adaptive equipment. Moreover the college, as well as the building being leased, has responsibilities under the ADA. Neither can evade its obligations by assuming the other will comply. The parties can agree to split the cost of renovations or adaptive equipment as long as the students have use of the pool, which is "as effective as" that provided to nondisabled students.

Program Access. The term *program access* derives from Section 504's provision that no person with a disability should be "subjected to discrimination under any program or activity" (29 U.S.C. sec. 794). Generally this term has been held to permit institutions to provide access to programs and activities without requiring extensive renovation or removal of architectural barriers. According to the regulations implementing Section 504, the term *program* includes housing, club activities, field trips, food service, counseling, transportation, and athletics. So when a university's cafeteria services were in an inaccessible location, OCR found the institution in violation of Section 504 (*University of Massachusetts, Amherst*, 1993).

Similarly, housing is a "program" under the regulations. OCR has found institutions in violation for failing to provide accessible housing, either because accessible housing was denied outright, or the level of access that a student needed was not evaluated on an individualized basis (*Southern Illinois University, Carbondale,* 1990).

When curb cuts are inaccessible, due to poor enforcement by university officials or a lack of adequate paving, OCR will find a violation. Similarly, where elevators are inoperable, the institution will be found in violation if that inoperable elevator excludes students from participation in sports or other activities (*Lawson State Community College,* 1993).

Physical barriers need not be the only barriers in housing programs. In *Coleman v. Zatechka* (1993), the housing department refused to assign a roommate to a student with cerebral palsy who used attendant care based on a policy premised on the notion that the roommate would not have sufficient space due to the presence of the attendant and Coleman's wheelchair and that the attendant would interfere with the roommate's right to privacy. The court found the university had erred in several ways. First, it did not conduct an individualized inquiry into whether Coleman would use more than her share of space or intrude on a roommate's privacy. Second, students who used wheelchairs but not attendants were not subject to this policy, although they also might use more space. The court also noted that the university did not police the use of space by other students who might have more personal belongings or simply monopolize the space. Third, the issues the university purported to address are the same issues all students face with roommates, regardless of disability.

Key Accommodation Provisions. A postsecondary educational institution must make reasonable accommodations in order to provide a student with a disability an equal opportunity to participate in the institution's courses, programs, and activities, including activities such as sports, fraternities and sororities, and clubs (*Wichita State University,* 1991). Students must provide adequate notice of disability. Once notified, however, the institution has an obligation to reasonably accommodate (*University of California, Los Angeles,* 1996), and it may not charge for reasonable accommodation, such as sign language interpreters or note takers (*Mercyhurst College,* 1997). By the same token, an institution need not provide accommodations that would fundamentally alter the educational program or academic requirements that are essential to a program of study (*Wong v. University of California,* 1999).

An institution is not responsible for providing personal services, such as attendants, hearing aids, or glasses (28 C.F.R. sec. 35.135). Under the applicable regulations, tutoring has been interpreted as a personal service and therefore need not be provided as an auxiliary aid or service. However, if a school provides tutoring to other students, it must make that tutoring program accessible to students with disabilities (*California State University, Sacramento,* 1996).

Many institutions have established remedial courses or programs to teach students with disabilities certain basic skills. Although these programs might be educationally important, they are not required by law. If an institution develops such programs, however, it must take care not to refuse to reasonably accommodate students who are taking these courses.

Auxiliary Aids and Services. An institution must provide auxiliary aids and services, such as qualified sign language interpreters, note takers, qualified readers, braille and large-print materials, and adaptive equipment (34 C.F.R. sec. 104.44, 28 C.F.R. sec. 35.104). A qualified interpreter is one who can communicate expressively and receptively, using any specialized vocabulary, in a manner that is effective, accurate, and impartial (28 C.F.R. sec. 35.105). Public institutions must give primary consideration to the requests of persons with disabilities and honor those requests unless the institution can demonstrate that another effective means of communication exists (28 C.F.R. sec. 35.160(b)).

Academic Adjustments. An institution must make academic adjustments to ensure that a student has an equal opportunity to participate in the institution's programs and activities (34 C.F.R. sec. 104.44(c)). Academic adjustments may include extended time for test taking, completion of course work, or graduation; tape recording of classes; substitution of specific courses to meet degree requirements; and modification of test taking or performance evaluation so as not to discriminate against a person's sensory, speaking, or motor impairments, except where such skills are the factors that the test purports to measure.

Students can be expected to take on a certain amount of responsibility for the securing of accommodations, such as asking a professor to identify a fellow student to take notes. However, where this is not successful, the institution must make sure that note-taking services are provided by some other means. Students are not to be left adrift because the system did not work. By the same token, the student is responsible for reporting to the disability services office that the established procedure did not work (*Solano Community College,* 1995).

Sometimes students fail to articulate adequately why the requested modification is needed and how their disability gives rise to this need. Few faculty or administrators are sufficiently knowledgeable about disabilities, particularly cognitive and psychiatric disabilities, to understand why the modification is requested. Nevertheless, institutions should orient their faculty to the requirements of the law and assist faculty to become knowledgeable about disabilities and how various disabilities can be appropriately accommodated.

Access to Computer Technology and the Internet. Colleges must ensure meaningful access to computer technology and the Internet. The OCR has advised that an "important indicator regarding the extent to which a public library is obligated to utilize adaptive technology is the degree to which it is relying on technology to serve its non-disabled patrons. . . . In other words, a library's decision to purchase technology of any kind, not only creates an expectation that the newly purchased technology will be accessible, but it suggests that the library now has the resources and expertise to fully consider the role of technology with regard to other aspects of its program" (*University of California, Los Angeles,* 1997). According to OCR "communication" means the "transfer of information, including (but not limited to) the verbal presentation of a lecturer, the printed text of a book and the resources of the Internet" (*California State University, Long Beach,* 1999).

Current Issues Regarding Students with Disabilities in Higher Education

As might be expected, compliance with the ADA has caused postsecondary institutions to reconsider how programs are administered and policies developed. As technology and our notions of civil rights evolve, certain issues have come to the fore. Some of the more pressing issues are described in this section.

Documentation. An unexpected result of the passage of the ADA is the erection of new hurdles that students with disabilities must vault to demonstrate that they have disabilities. This has taken the form of extensive documentation requirements, particularly for the so-called hidden disabilities, including learning disabilities, ADHD, and psychological disabilities.

The statute does not address documentation criteria, nor do the regulations. Nevertheless, legislative history and regulatory guidance demonstrate that Congress did not intend burdensome documentation requirements. Decisions about whether a person had a disability were not to be left to the sole discretion of the institutions.

Title III provides that "examinations and courses related to applications, licensing, certification, or credentialing for secondary or postsecondary education, professional or trade purposes" must be offered in a manner accessible to persons with disabilities (42 U.S.C. sec. 12189; 28 C.F.R. sec. 36.309). The Department of Justice noted that organizations that administer tests such as the Scholastic Achievement Test (SAT) "wanted to be able to require individuals with disabilities to provide advance notice and appropriate documentation, at the applicants' expense, of their disabilities and of any modifications or aids that would be required" (28 C.F.R. Part 36, Appendix B). The Department of Justice agreed that such requirements would be permissible, provided they were reasonable, "Documentation must be reasonable and limited to the need for the modification or aid requested. Appropriate documentation might include a letter from a physician or other professional, or evidence of a prior diagnosis or accommodation, such as eligibility for a special education program."

This limited guidance indicates the level of documentation required. Courts have addressed the issue of what documentation is needed and whose determination of disability carries more weight. In a number of cases, these decisions were made on the basis of motions filed by the defendants. The leading cases on this issue, however, are *Guckenberger v. Trustees of Boston University* (1997) and *Bartlett* (1997, 1998), both of which went to trial. In both cases, the courts held that the clinical judgment of the diagnosing professional is critical to the assessment of whether a person has a disability. The importance of clinical judgment was reinforced in *Wong v. Regents of the University of California* (1999) and *Doe v. National Board of Medical Examiners* (1999). An institution may not establish unduly burdensome documentation criteria or criteria that are inconsistent with accepted practice, especially where accepted practice requires clinical judgment. In *Bartlett,* the Second Circuit found that the Board of Law Examiners was not entitled to any deference in determining whether the plaintiff had a disability. The Board of Law Examiners had based its determination on theories that contravened accepted practice. The court found that although it had engaged a consultant to review documentation, the Board of Law Examiners had no expertise in determining disability, further noting that "even where an agency has expertise, courts should not allow agency factual determinations to go unchallenged" (*Bartlett,* p. 327).

Another documentation issue that has been the subject of extensive discussion is the recency of documentation. A university's determination that students with learning disabilities must be reassessed every three years in order to qualify for services was the precipitating event in *Guckenberger.* In that case, the university's president ordered that students must requalify for services every three years. This policy was fueled in large part by the president's belief that learning disabilities were "fugitive disorders" and that students with learning disabilities were "draft dodgers" (pp. 312, 315). The court found that because there was no research supporting the notion that learning disabilities do not continue into adulthood, and therefore no need to reassess a student for the presence of a learning disability every three years, this requirement was burdensome and discriminatory.

However, the court also found that the university was justified in requiring renewed documentation every three years of students with ADHD because the evidence at trial suggested that symptoms of ADHD could improve over time, and because many such students were under the care of physicians prescribing medication, this requirement would not be burdensome. Many psychologists and psychiatrists dispute that the evidence before the court reflected the most recent thinking about the nature of ADHD. Nevertheless *Guckenberger* demonstrates a case-by-case approach to documentation consistent with U.S. Supreme Court rulings because the *Guckenberger* court based its decision on the nature of each disability before it.

Conduct. Students with disabilities are not free to violate student codes of conduct simply because they have a disability; they must conduct themselves within the social and behavioral constraints of the academic community (*Arizona State University,* 1997). The most common problems occur when students engage in behaviors that are inconsistent with the social and professional norms of the relevant settings (*Doe v. New York University,* 1981). Permission to return to a university or an internship site often requires a certain level of appropriate conduct. The OCR has consistently refused to find these types of conditions to be violations of Section 504.

Access to Print and Alternate Text. Course materials must be available in alternate media at the start of the semester or, at a minimum, available when the relevant reading assignment is made. Handouts must be in alternate media when distributed to other students. Methods of note taking must be flexible, and institutions are responsible for providing certain equipment-related accommodations, including computers and tape recorders (*California Community Colleges,* 1996). An institution's policies and procedures may not result in a refusal or undue delay in services due to administrative convenience or otherwise (*Magill v. Iona College,* 1998).

When a student made a specific request for an upgrade to the university library's computer to permit him access, and the library both refused and failed to inform the student that he could use adaptive equipment located elsewhere on campus, OCR found the institution had violated Section 504 (*University of Oregon,* 1992). In *San Jose State University* (1997), OCR held that

> universit[ies] may, in appropriate circumstances, allocate or set priorities in use of resources consistent with the fundamental purpose of the University Library, but may not condition access to services, such as the microfiche collection, upon a showing of academic or course related relevance if those services are available to nondisabled students without such a showing. In short, in providing access, library staff may establish reasonable requirements for the provision of resources to provide access to services, such as requiring a student to make a prearranged appointment with a reader. . . . [Such] appointments . . . necessarily would be available during approximately the same hours and days that the library is available to others.

Colleges are therefore expected to keep up with technological advances. Access to the Internet has changed dramatically in recent years. Many institutions have been administratively slow to include students with disabilities when purchasing or upgrading computer equipment and software. Moreover OCR has found that the tendency of institutions to rely on a single centralized location for their adaptive computers has created numerous opportunities to isolate students with disabilities, which may be discriminatory (*California State University, Long Beach,* 1999).

Course Substitutions and Fundamental Alterations. Although the regulations list the substitution of courses for degree requirements as a possible academic adjustment, institutions need not do so if the courses are deemed essential to the student's program of study. Generally the courts defer to the institution's determination of essential requirements for an academic degree and other purely academic decisions. The courts and OCR repeatedly have refused to find a violation of Section 504 where the university was able to establish, through reasoned argument and analysis, that a course was essential to the institution's degree program, and particularly where the institution had made other reasonable accommodations for the complainant.

Nevertheless that deference is not absolute, as the U.S. Court of Appeals for the Ninth Circuit recently held. In *Wong v. University of California* (1999, p. 7), the court noted:

> Courts still hold the final responsibility for enforcing the Acts, including determining whether an individual is qualified, with or without accommodation, for the program in question. We must ensure that educational institutions are not "disguis[ing] truly discriminatory requirements" as academic decisions; to this end, [t]he educational institution has a real obligation . . . to seek suitable means of reasonably accommodating a handicapped person and to submit a factual record indicating that it conscientiously carried out this statutory obligation.

The OCR gave a detailed analysis regarding the issue of course substitutions and waivers, and the increasingly common problem of institutions' compelling students to take and fail basic skills courses repeatedly in order to demonstrate that a course substitution is warranted. Its determination in *Mt. San Antonio College* (1997) was uncannily like the court's in *Guckenberger.* In that case, OCR advised that the college not have an absolute, blanket policy of no course substitutions, but rather that it formally determine which core courses are fundamental to the granting of a degree from the institution or completion of a particular course of study and publish this determination widely. An institution should conduct a similar process in order to determine the reason that core courses are in the curriculum, the skills and principles that are among the goals to be attained through taking the core courses, and how those skills or principles can be inculcated using alternate means.

From a best-practices point of view, all stakeholders should be involved in the development of course substitution policies. Participants in that process should be cautioned to put aside preconceived notions to develop policy according to the letter and spirit of the ADA and Section 504. The establishment of course requirements that reflect nothing more than "I had to do it, so will you" is vulnerable to challenge.

Interpreters, Assistive Listening Devices, and Real-Time Captioning. In construing the conditions under which communication is as effective as that provided to nondisabled persons, on several occasions OCR has identified three basic components of effectiveness, "timeliness of delivery, accuracy of the translation, and provision in a manner and medium appropriate to the significance of the message and the abilities of the individual with a disability" (*University of California, Los Angeles,* 1997).

An institution must be diligent in providing these services. For example, if after making diligent efforts, a bona fide shortage of sign language interpreters results in the absence of interpreters for less than 10 percent of classes, the institution would not necessarily be in violation of the ADA or Section 504. However, effective alternatives must have been provided for those classes for which an interpreter was not present (*University of California, Davis*, 1992).

Diligent efforts presupposes that the institution's difficulty locating sign language interpreters is not a product of deliberate actions that result in an inability to locate qualified interpreters. In *College of the Redwoods* (1993), OCR found that the institution failed to make "diligent efforts" because it limited its search for interpreters to those in the immediate vicinity and its payments to less than half the market rate. In addition, OCR has also interpreted Title II's requirement that primary consideration be given to students' preferred methods of communication to encompass its previous position that note takers alone are insufficient to accommodate deaf students in higher education settings; note takers alone do not allow for communications that are as effective as those provided for nondisabled students (*San Diego Community College*, 1999).

Conclusion

It is in the best interests of all parties that decisions, policies, practices, and procedures are reviewed for compliance purposes with an open mind and an introspective analysis of the parties' preconceived notions about disability and higher education. A dose of common sense and a case-by-case review will go a long way toward ensuring both compliance with the laws and the meaningful participation of students with disabilities in higher education. The interactive process encouraged by the ADA is key to accommodating students with disabilities successfully. A truly interactive process ensures a proper balance among the rights and responsibilities of all parties. The Supreme Court's decisions in *Sutton, Murphy,* and *Albertsons* teach us that there are no absolutes in this endeavor, an important lesson.

References

Albertsons, Inc. v. Kirkingburg, 119 S. Ct. 2162 (1999).
Alexander v. Choate, 469 U.S. 287 (1985).
Arizona State University, 10 N.D.L.R 272 (OCR Region VIII, 1997).
Bartlett v. New York State Board of Law Examiners, 970 F. Supp. 1094 (S.D.N.Y. 1997).
     156 F.3d 321 (2d Cir. 1998), *vacated and remanded,* 119 S. Ct. 2388 (1999).
California Community Colleges, OCR Correspondence, Sept. 18, 1996.
California State University, Long Beach, OCR Case No. 09-99-2041 (Region IX, 1999).
California State University, Sacramento, OCR Case No. 09-95-2196 (Region VII, 1996).
Cleveland Chiropractic College, OCR Case No. 07-95-2051 (Region VII, 1995).
Coleman v. Zatechka, 824 F. Supp. 1360 (D. Nebr. 1993).
College of the Redwoods, OCR Case No. 09-93-2082-I (Region IX, 1993).

Doe v. National Board of Medical Examiners, No. C-993124 (N.D. Calif. 1999).

Doe v. New York University, 666 F.2d 761 (2d Cir. 1981).

Gonzalez v. National Board of Medical Examiners, 1999 WL 613434 (E.D. Mich. 1999).

Guckenberger v. Trustees of Boston University, 957 F. Supp. 306 (D. Mass. 1997); 974 F. Supp. 106 (D. Mass. 1997).

Lawson State Community College, 4 N.D.L.R. 449 (OCR Region IV, 1993).

Magill v. Board of Trustees of Iona College, 94 Civ. 9182 (S.D.N.Y. 1998).

Mercyhurst College, OCR Case No. 03-96-2188 (Region III, 1997).

Mt. San Antonio College, OCR Case No. 09-96-2151-I (Region IX, 1997).

Murphy v. United Parcel Service, Inc., 119 S. Ct. 2133 (1999).

Olmstead v. Zimring, 119 S. Ct. 2176 (1999).

Price v. National Board of Medical Examiners, 966 F. Supp. 419 (S.D. W. Va. 1997).

Pushkin v. Regents of the University of Colorado, 628 F.2d 1372 (10th Cir. 1981).

San Diego Community College, OCR Case Nos. 09-99-2078, 09-99-2095, 09-99-2104 (Region IX 1999).

San Jose State University, OCR Case No. 09-96-2056 (Region IX, 1997).

Soileau v. Maine, 105 F.3d 12 (1st Cir. 1997).

Solano Community College, OCR Case No. 09-94-2064-I (Region IX, 1995).

Southern Illinois University at Carbondale, 1 N.D.L.R. 143 (OCR Region V, 1990).

Sutton v. United Airlines, Inc., 119 S. Ct. 1752 (1999).

University of California, Davis, 4 N.D.L.R. 108 (OCR Region IX, 1992).

University of California, Los Angeles, 8 N.D.L.R. 314 (OCR Region IX, 1996).

University of California, Los Angeles, OCR Case No. 09-97-2002 (Region IX, 1997).

University of Massachusetts, Amherst, 4 N.D.L.R. 431 (OCR Region I, 1993).

University of Oregon, 3 N.D.L.R. 219 (OCR Region X, 1992).

University of Oregon, OCR Case No. 10962012 (Region X, 1996).

Wichita State University, 2 N.D.L.R. 154 (OCR Region VII, 1991).

Wong v. Regents of the University of California, 1999 WL 717729 (9th Cir. 1999).

Jo Anne Simon is an attorney in Brooklyn, New York, and is recognized for her work in disability law. She is an adjunct professor at Fordham University School of Law and serves on the board of directors of the Association on Higher Education and Disability.

7

Acknowledging historical precedent and fiscal and legislative constraints, how can postsecondary institutions best prepare for the future?

Funding Programs and Services for Students with Disabilities

James Rund, Tedde Scharf

In 1984, the American Council on Education (ACE) issued a statement on educational diversity, equality, and quality. That statement reiterated the commitment of higher education to these goals and in doing so called for the implementation of specific measures so that "minorities, women and disabled persons are able to enjoy full and equal participation in all aspects of institutional life" (p. 3). More recently, the Kellogg Commission issued a report on student access and noted, "Despite impressive progress in recent decades, educational opportunity in America is still far from equal. Full and equal access for all—to our institutions and to the full range of programs and services they provide—is a worthy and attainable goal. It remains to be met" (Kellogg Commission, 1998, p. 3). These statements, issued nearly fifteen years apart, articulate higher education's common and enduring commitment to access and equity in postsecondary education.

American higher education is admired in part because of the access it provides. Equitable access to higher education defines for many the opportunity to pursue their dreams and realize their potential. Higher education's commitment to diversity, equality, and quality is fundamental to its mission. Acknowledging the value of equitable access is paramount. Implementing strategies to achieve these ends may be a daunting challenge. Those who manage disability services and programs recognize the magnitude of this challenge and routinely struggle with one of the greatest barriers to equity and access—funding.

Key Funding Issues

The Rehabilitation Act of 1973, Section 504, and the Americans with Disabilities Act of 1990 (ADA) identify services essential for accommodating students with disabilities—readers, sign language and oral interpreters, note takers, lab science aides, and library research assistants. Since the ADA was passed in 1990, numerous court cases and U.S. Department of Education Office of Civil Rights (OCR) complaint resolutions have held institutions responsible for providing appropriate accommodations. Today most colleges and universities readily accept this responsibility. As a result, most institutions have an office of disability services staffed by qualified professionals prepared to ensure compliance with federal law and to determine and facilitate the provision of appropriate accommodations (American Association of Community Colleges, 1999).

Disability accommodations require adequate funding. In some cases, institutions are tempted to select accommodations based on cost or administrative convenience. The OCR has never ruled in favor of an institution of higher education that claimed undue financial hardship as a reason for not providing disability accommodations. Institutions do have options in providing effective accommodations as long as they have consulted with the student, researched available accommodations, and considered the student's preference.

Some disability accommodations, such as sign language interpreting or services for visually impaired students, require substantial financial investment. Specialized equipment, hardware, software, and technical personnel are expensive ongoing costs, as are mandated auxiliary aides such as note takers, readers, interpreters, library research aides, and science lab assistants.

Current Concerns

Higher education and its liaisons in state and federal government have debated for years the intent of Section 504 of the Rehabilitation Act of 1973 and related sections of the Higher Education Act of 1965, the 1998 Amendments to the Act, and the Americans with Disabilities Act of 1990 (Postsecondary Education Programs Network, 1999). The fundamental question over time has remained, Who pays?

The Rehabilitation Act Amendments of 1998 made changes to and reauthorized the Vocational Rehabilitation Act of 1973. The amendment mandates that state agencies, including colleges and universities, "work together to devise a plan for determining financial responsibility for services provided to clients of VR agencies who are enrolled in post-secondary education" (HEATH, 1999, p. 2). More specifically, plans are to be developed at the state level to determine who provides and pays for specific accommodations.

This mandated cooperation between postsecondary institutions and state agencies is likely to be challenged because historic precedents are difficult to reverse. Meanwhile students will continue to enroll in record numbers. *The Condition of Education 1998* (U.S. Department of Education, 1998) reported that the number of K–12 students who participated in federal programs for students with disabilities increased 51 percent between 1977 and 1996. The report also indicated that those who received this support represented 12 percent of the total enrollment in public schools compared to 8 percent in 1977. The HEATH Resource Center (1995) indicated that 9.2 percent of freshmen in 1994 reported having some type of disability, compared to 2.6 percent in 1978. Of this group, one-third reported having a learning disability. Students reporting learning disabilities doubled from 1988 to 1994, and this growth trend is expected to continue.

Sources of Funding

Growing numbers of students and increasing pressure to leverage funding at the local, state, and federal levels create unique challenges for disability programs. Historically, various fund sources (federal, state, institutional) have been relied on to support students with disabilities. Although the categories or types of funds have not changed dramatically over time, managing the effective disbursement of funds is an increasingly complex challenge.

Federal Funds. The greatest sources of support for disability programs are federal initiatives. Federal legislation has historically provided base funding for thousands of programs. When the Rehabilitation Act of 1973 was signed in 1977, the issue of primary responsibility for funding accommodations was addressed directly in the law (Postsecondary Education Programs Network, 1999). Vocational rehabilitation (VR) primarily served individuals with physical disabilities. Section 504 created a plethora of professional job training opportunities for the severely disabled through higher education. VR paid for auxiliary aids such as interpreters, braille production, readers, and equipment (for example, wheelchairs, braces, and hearing and visual aids). However, by the time ADA was signed into law in 1990, the number of persons with disabilities served by VR had increased dramatically. Costs had also risen sharply with the inclusion of expensive technology required to assist and retrain individuals with disabilities.

Realizing the extensive funding required of the 1990 legislation, the U.S. Congress excluded funding to states, institutions, and public or private programs. Initially this seemed adverse to the intent of the law, but it ultimately forced all parties to meet the legal requirements and budget for these mandates over a multiyear process. Institutions of higher learning fared better than other public or private entities due to a thirteen-year head start initiated by the passage of Section 504 legislation in 1977. Through the Reauthorization of Higher Education, students with disabilities were added to the disadvantaged and minority groups covered by the U.S. Department of Education TRIO funding for Student Support Services, Upward Bound, and the Educational Opportunity Center grants. This inclusion provided some limited funding for accommodations in community colleges and four-year institutions of higher education. Succeeding rehabilitation reauthorization acts have provided training and program development funds for at-risk population areas such as the deaf, deaf and blind, and blind.

Multiple federal agencies, including the Department of Education, the Department of Health and Human Services, and the Department of Housing and Urban Development, channel funds to disability programs. Federal grants also provide an ample source of funding where federal dollars are often used to match postsecondary funds to address specific institutional needs. Grants from the Office of Special Education, the Veterans Administration, the Department of Justice, and the National Institutes of Health have supported campus-based programs with critical funding to address unique needs and meet standards of compliance.

More recent federal funding has also been made available through the National Science Foundation (NSF). These grants fund the research and development of teaching methodologies for students with disabilities and the technology that makes access to the science fields possible. NSF actively solicits grant applications that include disability issues in some form.

State Funds. Not unlike federal dollars, state funds are essential in addressing fundamental program needs and assisting campuses in responding to local or regional priorities. State agency funding often augments federal support by enhancing programs that serve the special needs of the state. State allocations in some instances are used as incentive funds to provide critical services or begin new programs. State agencies also provide opportunities for partnering. State vocational rehabilitation programs and related agencies figure significantly in financial planning for campus programs. The financial challenges that these programs face are frequently similar to those that state agencies face. While this may prompt competition for funds in some instances, it also provides the opportunity for liaisons to be developed and partnerships forged.

Community Funds. An increasing number of campus programs are turning to partners and advocates in their local communities for assistance. Community support comes in many forms—volunteered time, money, equipment, or advocacy. Private sector support and corporate partnerships are rapidly growing in scope and frequency, often where sustained goals can be advanced—the hiring and training of a diversified workforce; the development of new products or services; and the social and economic development of a community, city, or state. Private foundations and nonprofit organizations also have discovered that campus disability programs can be beneficial groups with which to associate because gifted funds are prudently managed, easily accounted for, and used to produce tangible results.

Institutional Funds. Institutional funds are perhaps the greatest variable in program funding. Campus support varies dramatically and is greatly influenced by institutional type, size, and student demographics. Institutional support is made available in various forms—capital funds for facilities renovation, base funding for personnel or operating costs, and one-time funds for equipment upgrades or unanticipated needs. Given the limited amount and discretion of institutional funds, support for campus programs has generally remained static over the past several years.

Issues Related to Funding

Successful funding of disability programs is often contingent on flexibility in financing program requirements, accounting for variables in financial planning, and effectively executing the program budget. Several conditions complicate the funding scenario and these are chief among them.

Flexibility. Funding programs through multiple fund sources for some budget analysts suggest great flexibility and perhaps even adequate support. In reality, the opposite is more typical. Federal funds, which often provide base funding for new programs, are often prescriptive in nature and therefore narrowly applied. This is especially true with federal grants, where awards follow a competitive proposal process driven by specific criteria and stringent guidelines.

Targeted or earmarked funds present several unique challenges in administering effective disability programs. Funds are often requested for an explicit purpose and must be expended to address the expressed need. Programs lack the flexibility to adjust funds to meet program needs and are restricted in their ability to use funds most effectively.

Planning and Budgeting. The variables in planning introduced by multiple fund sources, origin, and nature of funds make budgeting complex and difficult. The variables in student demographics, or clients served, compound the difficulty in planning and budgeting. The number of students requesting support from disability programs may fluctuate greatly from one year to the next. The number of students requesting specific services or accommodations may also vary greatly, even when aggregate numbers are constant. Program administrators are faced with significant challenges in meeting service demands and maintaining compliance standards while expending funds congruent with the respective requirements.

Grant funds, as an example, are often pursued as a means of offsetting costs that the campus incurs to support disability services. In a given year, grant funds may be more than adequate to cover personnel and operating costs for a particular program component. With program costs per student in some cases exceeding $20,000 annually, unanticipated student increases, even when moderate, may easily overextend a budget.

Prudent Management

The administration of public funds rarely involves incentives for high productivity or efficiency. The prevailing approach is to secure the funds necessary, expend them within the respective and appropriate time period, ensure against any unspent funds to avoid the perception of overfunding, and repeat the cycle the following year.

Little motivation exists for program managers to cut costs when feasible, share costs when appropriate, or save funds when possible. Program managers have few opportunities to leverage program funding for any purpose, immediate or future. Prudent fiscal management nets few rewards and in some instances has resulted only in reduced funding in subsequent years.

These conditions are not new to program administrators, and although several effective strategies have been developed to manage these complex issues, the following examples represent many of the best practices employed by disability programs today.

Arizona State University. Arizona State University (ASU) is a public university located in metropolitan Phoenix. The university enrolls forty-five thousand students and serves more than thirteen hundred students with disabilities through its Disability Resources for Students (DRS) program. The DRS program employs more than eighteen full-time and thirty-four part-time staff who provide comprehensive disability services, including sign language interpreting, real-time captioning, mobility services, C-print operators, reading services, braille and alternative print format production, and coordination for in-class accommodations.

ASU partners with state, county, and local agencies, vocational rehabilitation, and local businesses to provide programs to students with disabilities. Funding sources include a U.S. Department of Education TRIO Student Support Services grant, private donations, corporate sponsorships, and university funds. Hewlett-Packard has funded an adaptive technology center that serves as a comprehensive facility for students with a variety of physical and cognitive disabilities. DRS awards $100,000 a year in scholarships to students with disabilities.

Blue Ridge Community College. Blue Ridge Community College, located in North Carolina, enrolls approximately seventeen hundred students. The college created a Special Populations Office in 1991 to support students with disabilities. Approximately two hundred students with disabilities register and use services each year through the office, which is staffed by one full-time professional and one part-time assistant. Traditional funding sources include federal and state funds as well as support from the Blue Ridge Community College Foundation.

Private funding, volunteers, and local partnerships supplement the office's funding. A grant from the Melvin R. Lane Charitable Trust funded an accessible computer lab. Blue Ridge student volunteers take notes for students with disabilities, and Phi Theta Kappa members volunteer tutorial support. Local health care professionals make presentations to college faculty on topics related to disabilities to enhance awareness and increase support for students with disabilities.

Columbus State Community College. Columbus State Community College, located in Columbus, Ohio, offers a Department of Disability Services for students with disabilities. The program, in existence since 1972, currently serves more than four hundred students with disabilities; the college's total enrollment is approximately twenty thousand students. A staff of eleven full-time employees and thirty-five part-time employees provides a full range of services and resources to students with disabilities. The college, which draws a large number of deaf and hard-of-hearing students, has had four full-time interpreters on staff since the mid-1980s.

As funding from external sources, such as Vocational Rehabilitation and Perkins, diminished in previous years, the college began to rely on internal funding mechanisms and now funds its entire disability services program. Supplemental funding comes from the state Board of Regents as reimbursement for services provided to students with disabilities. The college generally uses these unrestricted funds to pay for real-time services and new assistive technology or facility upgrades.

Vanderbilt University. Vanderbilt University, a private university located in Nashville, Tennessee, runs its disability services program through the Opportunity Development Center, which oversees all equal opportunity and affirmative action programs and unlawful discrimination complaints, in addition to ADA compliance and disability services for university employees and students. The program serves nearly three hundred students with disabilities; the university's enrollment is near eleven thousand. The disability program was established in 1979 and has three full-time and three part-time staff.

Traditional funding sources primarily include institutional support, with some vocational rehabilitation support. The disability program also shares costs with academic colleges, if colleges are able to share in the costs of providing service to their students. The department partners with the Peabody College of Education to share equipment and use the resources of faculty and graduate students for programs such as campus orientation. Through partnerships with local organizations, the office has written grants to purchase new equipment.

Vanderbilt has a mechanism in place that makes policy recommendations regarding disability issues, some of which may have funding implications. The Equal Access Committee, which reports to the chancellor and is composed of faculty, staff, and students, evaluates issues related to accessibility and makes recommendations to the chancellor. The chancellor's office provides funding for any costs associated with implementing the recommendations.

A Continuing Dilemma

While the success of some programs will encourage and motivate others, disability programs will continue to face challenges in funding. Programs supported by public funds will always struggle for funding because budget requests for mandates or compliance standards rarely garner support for relevant funding. Even institutions that address their obligations for disability services often do so reluctantly. Recasting disability programs may help in this regard, encouraging different thinking, more enlightened perspectives, and perhaps even more funding. Through implementation of creative approaches, cultivation of key constituents, and education of the campus community, disability programs can achieve funding objectives and program goals.

Educate. Campuses are places that welcome discussion and debate. Generating a campus dialogue on disability issues will serve as a vehicle to educate. Exposure to information, people, and differing perspectives can be a powerful way to accomplish this. Educating colleagues about the needs, interests, and desires of others can generate support and solidarity. Campuses can be transformed into inclusive environments where all individuals are acknowledged, encouraged, and supported in their endeavors. The more a campus community is aware of and informed about disabled students, the more enriched it becomes.

A strategy for educating. To secure greater financial support, some disability program administrators have prevailed on their senior administration and budget officers to lobby legislators or policymakers. Bringing these decision makers to campus and providing them access to programs and students through tours and interviews can be an effective way to influence funding decisions. Humanizing the fiscal implications of what legislators regard as a government mandate may be beneficial to everyone. This interaction enlightens the uninformed and makes real the abstract dimension of the requirements.

Cultivate. Exposure to people and information is important, as are relationships and liaisons. Campus advocates for disability services should be identified, made aware of the issues involved in problem solving, and participate in planning and budgeting. Campus advocates should be familiar with program strengths as well as areas that need improvement. Advocates should also be relied on to broaden the base of support with campus colleagues and, where relevant, develop contacts in the community.

A strategy for cultivating. Budget processes vary greatly from campus to campus, but critical decision makers are common to all. Knowing the decision makers, garnering their support, and connecting them to others helps build momentum and increase support for disability programs. Faculty advocates, business managers, facilities managers, campus planners, and student service personnel should be sought out as advocates to enhance the campus through disability programs. Involvement from senior leadership can also be useful to secure a commitment for the campus environment to treat all students with dignity and respect. Because transforming a campus requires broad participation, other campus leaders should be relied on to support and promote disability programs. This involvement may not prevail in every budget cycle, but it will generate positive inertia and sustainable progress.

Be Creative. Sometimes the biggest problem in securing funding and advancing a program is lack of creativity. The cyclical nature of budget processes can contribute to a staid and patterned way of administering. Assumptions are made about what can and cannot be done, at times based more on history or perceptions of reality than reality itself. The incremental and rudimentary elements of requesting and expending funds reinforce historical precedent. Yet students change, as do their needs, and disability programs must develop ways to remain current and contemporary.

A strategy for being creative. If disability programs have historically been constrained by limited flexibility, what alternatives exist to change that? If public budgeting provides disincentives for prudent resource management, what can be done to alter that? Campuses do have discretion in these areas, and options do exist, especially where the alternative may benefit both the disabilities program and the campus at large. New initiatives or alternatives should be considered. Expanded or enhanced services, for example, can be offered in exchange for more or different sources of financial support (or both). A carry-forward balance in one budget year provides the option of offering assistance to other departments in exchange for greater institutional support in more difficult budget times. Perhaps more than any other attribute, strong disability programs approach conventional problems in creative and sometimes unconventional ways. This strategy benefits students, strengthens programs, and enhances campus environments.

Conclusion

The Rehabilitation Act of 1973, the Higher Education Act of 1965, the recent amendments to both, and the ADA legislation of 1990 all contributed to the origination and growth of disability programs. Improvements long overdue and new initiatives never before contemplated have improved the lives of thousands who are pursuing their goals in higher education.

Corrective action, legislatively mandated, stigmatizes programs and ultimately those who are served by them. After nearly three decades, perhaps it is time for institutions to move away from the mandate mind-set and closer to the principles of equality and access, from a sense of obligation to a sense of responsibility, from a need to be compliant to a desire to fulfill a commitment.

Language in these matters is important. It offers perspective and shapes behavior. This can be extraordinarily important in matters of funding where needs are often defined and financially supported or rejected based on bias or perspective.

Several programs across the country have begun this process of change, generating ever increasing support for their programs as they inform and educate those around them. Informed perspectives shape priorities, and there will always be support for what is deemed most important.

References

American Association of Community Colleges. "Disability Support Services National Survey." [http: //www.aacc.nche.edu/initiatives/DISSRVCS/survey.htm]. May 1999.

American Council on Education. *Statement on Educational Diversity, Equality, and Quality. Self-Regulation Initiatives: Guidelines for Colleges and Universities* (No. 9). Washington, D.C.: American Council on Education, 1984.

HEATH Resource Center. "College Freshmen with Disabilities." *Information from HEATH,* 1995, *14*(2, 3).

HEATH Resource Center. "Recent Legislative Developments in Postsecondary Education and Disability." [http://www.acenet.edu/about/programs/Acc. . ./1999/02february/recnt_legilation.html]. Feb. 9, 1999.

Kellogg Commission. *Returning to Our Roots: Student Access.* Washington, D.C.: National Association of State Universities and Land-Grant Colleges, 1998.

Postsecondary Education Programs Network. "1998 Amendments to Section 504 of the Rehabilitation Act of 1973: Interagency Agreements." [http://www.pepnet.org]. Jul. 1999.

U.S. Department of Education. Office of Educational Research and Improvement. National Center for Education Statistics. *The Condition of Education.* Washington, D.C.: U.S. Department of Education, 1998.

JAMES RUND is associate vice president for student affairs and affiliated professor in educational leadership and policy studies at Arizona State University in Tempe.

TEDDE SCHARF is associate director of disability services for students at Arizona State University in Tempe.

Name Index

Subject Index

Admissions process, 34–38
Americans with Disabilities Act (ADA), 6, 34, 42, 43, 57, 69–73, 76, 79, 80, 84, 85
Arizona State University, 88
Attitudinal barriers, 12, 50, 60–61

Ball State University, 44
Blue Ridge Community College, 88

Campus environments: communal, 27–28; conclusions about, 28; human aggregate components of, 21, 24–25; involving, 25–27; and Maslow's hierarchy of needs, 23; organizational components of, 21–22, 25; physical components, 20–21, 24; safe and inclusive, 23–25; social climate of, 22, 25; and "social constructivism," 19–20
Career and academic advising issues: and assumptions about disabilities, 58–59; and atmosphere of trust, 58, 59–60; barriers facing students, 58, 60–61; creative problem solving for, 58, 61–63; disclosure of disability, 58, 63; fostering of student's independence, 58, 64–65; and interactional model, 55–57; student's focus on disability, 58, 63–64
Columbus State Community College, 88–89
Community as a value, 1, 2, 10, 11
Course materials, 78
Course substitutions and alterations, 78–79

Demographic trends, 7–9
Disclosure of disability, 34, 36, 63
DO-IT CAREERS project, 46
Documentation of disability, 76–77

Education of All Handicapped Children Act (Public Law 94-142), 31, 36
Environments, campus: communal, 27–28; conclusions about, 28; human aggregate components of, 21, 24–25; involving, 25–27; and Maslow's hierarchy of needs, 23; organizational components of, 21–22, 25; physical

components, 20–21, 24; safe and inclusive, 23–25; social climate of, 22, 25; and "social constructivism," 19–20
Equality as a value, 1–2, 10, 11

Family Educational Rights and Privacy Act, 72
Funding for disability programs: at Arizona State University, 88; as barrier to equity, 83–84; at Blue Ridge Community College, 88; at Columbus State Community College, 88–89; complications of, 87; concerns about, 84–85; conclusions about, 91; creativity in securing, 91; sources of, 85–87; at Vanderbilt University, 89

Hiring practices on campuses, 14
Human dignity, 1, 2, 10–11

Individuals with Disabilities Education Act (IDEA), 72–73
Interactional model of disability: applying, 57–65; and approaches to student services, 56–57; and student development theory, 55–56
International exchange programs, 46–49
Internships, 44–45
Interpreters, sign language, 79–80
Involving environments, 25–27

Legal issues: access to course materials, 78; course substitutions and alterations, 78–79; documentation of disability, 76–77; interpreters, 79–80; student conduct, 77–78
Legal mandates: access to postsecondary education under, 73–76; Americans with Disabilities Act (ADA), 6, 34, 42, 43, 57, 69–73, 76, 79, 80, 84, 85; Family Educational Rights and Privacy Act, 72; general obligations, 69–71; Individuals with Disabilities Education Act (IDEA), 72–73; Section 504 of Rehabilitation Act of 1973, 5, 6, 31, 34, 36–37, 42–43, 57, 69–70, 71, 72–73, 78, 79, 80, 84, 85; who is protected under, 71–72

Back Issue/Subscription Order Form

Copy or detach and send to:
Jossey-Bass Publishers, 350 Sansome Street, San Francisco CA 94104-1342

Call or fax toll free!
Phone 888-378-2537 6AM–5PM PST; Fax 800-605-2665

Back issues: Please send me the following issues at $23 each
(Important: please include series initials and issue number, such as SS90)

1. SS _____

_____

_____

$ _____ Total for single issues

$ _____ Shipping charges (for single issues *only;* subscriptions are exempt
from shipping charges): Up to $30, add $5^{50} • $30^{01}–$50, add $6^{50}
$50^{01}–$75, add $8 • $75^{01}–$100, add $10 • $100^{01}–$150, add $12
Over $150, call for shipping charge

Subscriptions   Please ❏ start   ❏ renew my subscription to *New Directions for
Student Services* for the year _____ at the following rate:

U.S.   ❏ Individual $58   ❏ Institutional $104
Canada: ❏ Individual $83   ❏ Institutional $129
All Others: ❏ Individual $88   ❏ Institutional $134
NOTE: Subscriptions are quarterly, and are for the calendar year only.
Subscriptions begin with the Spring issue of the year indicated above.

$ _____ Total single issues and subscriptions (Add appropriate sales tax for
your state for single issue orders. No sales tax for U.S. subscriptions. NY
and Canadian residents, add GST for subscriptions and single issues.)

❏ Payment enclosed (U.S. check or money order only)

❏ VISA, MC, AmEx, Discover Card # _____ Exp. date_____

Signature _____ Day phone _____

❏ Bill me (U.S. institutional orders only. Purchase order required.)

Purchase order #_____

Federal Tax ID 135593032   GST 89102-8052

Name _____

Address _____

_____

Phone_____ E-mail _____

For more information about Jossey-Bass Publishers, visit our Web site at:
www.josseybass.com   **PRIORITY CODE = ND1**

DATE DUE

ILL (MTG)		
3071(6l3)		
6/13/07		